WORLD IN CONFLICT

TIBET

DISPUTED LAND

TIBET

DISPUTED LAND

by Peter Kizilos

Lerner Publications Company / Minneapolis

Lerner Publications Company
A division of Lerner Publishing Group
241 First Avenue North
Minneapolis, MN 55401 U.S.A.

Website address: www.lernerbooks.com

All maps by Philip Schwartzberg, Meridian Mapping, Minneapolis.
Cover photo © Dermot Tatlow/Panos Pictures
Table of contents photos (from top to bottom) by: © Dermot Tatlow/
Panos Pictures, © Don Farber/Sygma, © Steve Lehman, © Kurt Thorson.

Series Consultant: Andrew Bell-Fialkoff
Editorial Director: Mary M. Rodgers
Editors: Kari Cornell, Lisa K. McCallum
Designer: Mike Tacheny
Photo Researcher: Cheryl Hulting

LIBRARY OF CONGRESS CATALOGING-IN-PUBLICATION DATA

Kizilos, Peter.
    Tibet : disputed land / by Peter Kizilos.
        p.   cm. — (World in conflict)
    Includes index.
    Summary: Examines the history of the ethnic conflict in Tibet and its continuing effect on the people.
        ISBN 0-8225-3563-7 (lib. bdg.)
        1. Tibet (China)—History—1951– —Juvenile literature. 2. Tibet (China)—Civilization—Juvenile literature. [1. Tibet (China)—History.] I. Series.
    DS786.K578 2000
    951'.5—dc21   98-54083

Manufactured in the United States of America
1 2 3 4 5 6 – JR – 05 04 03 02 01 00

CONTENTS

ABOUT THIS SERIES

Government firepower kills 25 protesters . . . . Thousands of refugees flee the country . . . . Rebels attack capital . . . . Racism and rage flare . . . . Fighting breaks out . . . . Peace talks stall . . . . Bombing toll rises to 52 . . . . Slaughter has cost up to 50,000 lives.

Conflicts between people occur across the globe, and we hear about some of the more spectacular and horrific episodes in the news. But since most fighting doesn't directly affect us, we often choose to ignore it. And even if we do take the time to learn about these conflicts—from newspapers, magazines, television news, or radio—we're often left with just a snapshot of the conflict instead of the whole reel of film.

Most news accounts don't tell you the whole story about a conflict, focusing instead on the attention-grabbing events that make the headlines. In addition, news sources may have a preconceived idea about who is right and who is wrong in a conflict. The stories that result often portray one side as the "bad guys" and the other as the "good guys."

The *World in Conflict* series approaches each conflict with the idea that wars and political disputes aren't simply about bullies and victims. Conflicts are complex problems that can often be traced back hundreds of years. The people fighting one another have complicated reasons for doing so. Fighting erupts between groups divided by ethnicity, religion, and nationalism. These groups fight over power, money, territory, control. Sometimes people who just want to go about their own business get caught up in a conflict just because they're there.

These books examine major conflicts around the world, some of which are very bloody and others that haven't involved a lot of violence. They portray the people involved in and affected by conflicts. They describe how each conflict got started, how it developed, and where it stands. The books also outline some of the ways people have tried to end the conflicts. By reading the stories behind the headlines, you will learn some reasons why people hate and fight one another and, in addition, why some people struggle so hard to end conflicts.

WORDS YOU NEED TO KNOW

amban: A civil officer, first appointed by the Chinese emperor in the early 1700s, who was to report to Beijing about events in Lhasa.

annex: To incorporate a region into a country or territory.

Buddhism: A religion of eastern and central Asia derived from the teachings of Siddhartha Gautama Buddha who believed that suffering is part of life and that in order for Buddhists to become free from suffering, they must purify themselves through prayer and ritual.

civil disobedience: Refusing to obey governmental orders or laws through nonviolent means. This form of protest is most effective when a large group of people take part.

commune: The highest administrative level in China's rural regions from 1958 until the mid-1980s. Each commune had its own government and economy, producing either crops or manufactured goods for the state.

communist: A person who supports communism—an economic system in which the government owns the means of producing goods in factories and of growing food.

Cultural Revolution: A period spanning the years 1966 to 1976 when Mao Zedong encouraged the masses to rebel against traditional society and to adopt communist ideals. Students, who came to be known as Red Guards, acted as soldiers for Mao, destroying religious temples and harassing university professors and other intellectuals.

dissident: A person who disagrees with an established religious or political system, organization, or belief.

ethnic group: A permanent group of people bonded together by a combination of cultural markers.

infrastructure: The system of roads, schools, and other resources used by the public and maintained by the government of the country, state, or region.

martial law: Authority that an occupying force imposes upon the occupied territory in emergency situations when the civilian law enforcement divisions cannot control the public.

propaganda: Ideas, rumors, or information spread to influence people's opinion. The intent of propaganda may be either to injure or to promote an institution, a cause, or a people.

refugee: A person who leaves his or her home country to escape hardship or persecution.

regional autonomy: The right and power of a region—usually characterized by a shared set of cultural markers, economy, and history—to govern itself.

separatism: A movement by a group of people towards independence or autonomy.

sinicize: To make something, such as culture or architecture, become more Chinese.

sovereignty: Power over a region.

Tibetan Buddhism: A form of Buddhism practiced in Tibet. Since Buddhism was introduced in Tibet in A.D. 630, it has become central to Tibetan culture. Over time, Tibetans have added their own beliefs and traditions to the religion.

FOREWORD

by Andrew Bell-Fialkoff

Conflicts between various groups are as old as time. Peoples and tribes around the world have fought one another for thousands of years. In fact our history is in great part a succession of wars—between the Greeks and the Persians, the English and the French, the Russians and the Poles, and many others. Not only do states or ethnic groups fight one another, so do followers of different religions—Catholics and Protestants in Northern Ireland, Christians and Muslims in Bosnia, and Buddhists and Hindus in Sri Lanka. Often ethnicity, language, and religion—some of the main distinguishing elements of culture—reinforce one another in characterizing a particular group. For instance, the vast majority of Greeks are Orthodox Christian and speak Greek; most Italians are Roman Catholic and speak Italian. Elsewhere, one cultural aspect predominates. Serbs and Croats speak dialects of the same language but remain separate from one another because most Croats are Catholics and most Serbs are Orthodox Christians. To those two groups, religion is more important than language in defining culture.

We have witnessed an increasing number of conflicts in modern times—why? Three reasons stand out. One is that large empires—such as Austria-Hungary, Ottoman Turkey, several colonial empires with vast holdings in Asia, Africa, and America, and, most recently, the Soviet Union—have collapsed. A look at world maps from 1900, 1950, and 1998 reveals an ever-increasing number of small and medium-sized states. While empires existed, their rulers suppressed many ethnic and religious conflicts. Empires imposed order, and local resentments were mostly directed at the central authority. Inside the borders of empires, populations were multiethnic and often highly mixed. When the empires fell apart, world leaders found it impossible to establish political frontiers that coincided with ethnic boundaries. Different groups often claimed territories inhabited by others. The nations created on the lands of a toppled empire were saddled with acute border and ethnic problems from their very beginnings.

The second reason for more conflicts in modern times stems from the twin ideals of freedom and equality. In the United States, we usually think of freedom as "individual freedom." If we all have equal rights, we are free. But if you are a member of a minority group and feel that you are being discriminated against, your group's rights and freedoms are also important to you. In fact, if you don't have your "group freedom," you don't have full individual freedom either.

After World War I (1914–1918), the allied western nations, under the guidance of U.S. president Woodrow Wilson, tried to satisfy group rights by promoting minority rights. The spread of frantic nationalism in the 1930s, especially among disaffected ethnic minorities, and the catastrophe of World War II (1939–1945) led to a fundamental reassessment of the Wilsonian philosophy. After 1945 group rights were downplayed on the assumption that guaranteeing individual rights would be sufficient. In later decades, the collapse of multiethnic nations like Czechoslovakia, Yugoslavia, and the Soviet Union—coupled with the spread of nationalism in those regions—came as a shock to world leaders. People want democracy and individual rights, but they want their group rights, too. In practice, this means more conflicts and a cycle of secession, as minority ethnic groups seek their own sovereignty and independence.

The fires of conflict are often further stoked by the media, which lavishes glory and attention on independence movements. To fight for freedom is an honor. For every Palestinian who has killed an Israeli, there are hundreds of Kashmiris, Tamils, and Bosnians eager to shoot at their enemies. Newspapers, television and radio news broadcasts, and other media play a vital part in fomenting that sense of honor. They magnify each crisis, glorify rebellion, and help to feed the fire of conflict.

The third factor behind increasing conflict in the world is the social and geographic mobility that modern society enjoys. We can move anywhere we want and can aspire—or so we believe—to be anything we wish. Every day the television tantalizingly dangles the prizes that life can offer. We all want our share. But increased mobility and ambition also mean increased competition, which leads to antagonism. Antagonism often fastens itself to ethnic, racial, or religious differences. If you are an inner-city African American and your local grocer happens to be Korean American, you may see that individual as different from yourself—an intruder—rather than as a person, a neighbor, or a grocer. This same feeling of "us" versus "them" has been part of many an ethnic conflict around the world.

Many conflicts have been contained—even solved—by wise, responsible leadership. But unfortunately, many politicians use citizens' discontent for their own ends. They incite hatred, manipulate voters, and mobilize people against their neighbors. The worst things happen when neighbor turns against neighbor. In Bosnia, in Rwanda, in Lebanon, and in countless other places, people who had lived and worked together and had even intermarried went on a rampage, killing, raping, and robbing one another with gusto. If the appalling carnage teaches us anything, it is that we should stop seeing one another as hostile competitors and enemies and accept one another as people. Most importantly, we should learn to understand why conflicts happen and how they can be prevented. That is why *World in Conflict* is so important—the books in this series will help you understand the history and inner dynamics of some of the most persistent conflicts of modern times. And understanding is the first step to prevention. ⊕

INTRODUCTION

For centuries, adventurers and explorers from around the world have traveled to Tibet, which lies in a mountainous region in south central Asia. Tibet is known to most as the home of Mount Everest—the highest mountain on earth. The region's high elevation, treacherous mountain passes, and blinding blizzards have earned Tibet nicknames such as "The Roof of the World" and "The Land of Snows."

Until the middle of the twentieth century, Tibet was relatively isolated from the rest of the world. Most Tibetans were farmers or herders. **Tibetan Buddhism,** a religion based on the belief that after death people experience a series of reincarnations or rebirths, played a central role in Tibetan life. High-ranking Tibetan monks controlled monasteries that served as centers for learning and culture. Monasteries often perched on extensive plots of land that monks divided and rented to peasant farmers. The farmers practiced subsistence farming, meaning that they could keep some produce for themselves but were required to give the rest to the head of the estate. Noble families also held large estates and rented parcels of land to peasant farmers.

CLASH OF CULTURES

Big changes came to Tibet when armies of the People's Republic of China (PRC) arrived in 1950. Communist troops had just won the revolution in China and were reestablishing Chinese territory. According to the Chinese, Tibet had been part of China since the thirteenth century when Mongol invaders had united the two regions. By taking over Tibet, China was just grabbing hold of land that it had controlled for hundreds of years. Within a year, the Chinese had overthrown the local government and had **annexed** Tibet, making it a Chinese province.

As a part of China, Tibet became swept up in the economic and cultural changes that the PRC imposed on the entire country. The government seized large estates and redistributed the land into group farms called **communes**. To increase productivity, the government established work brigades.

Facing page: *The Chinese province of Tibet, or Tibet Autonomous Region (TAR), is neighbor to Nepal and India and home to most of the Himalayan mountain range.*

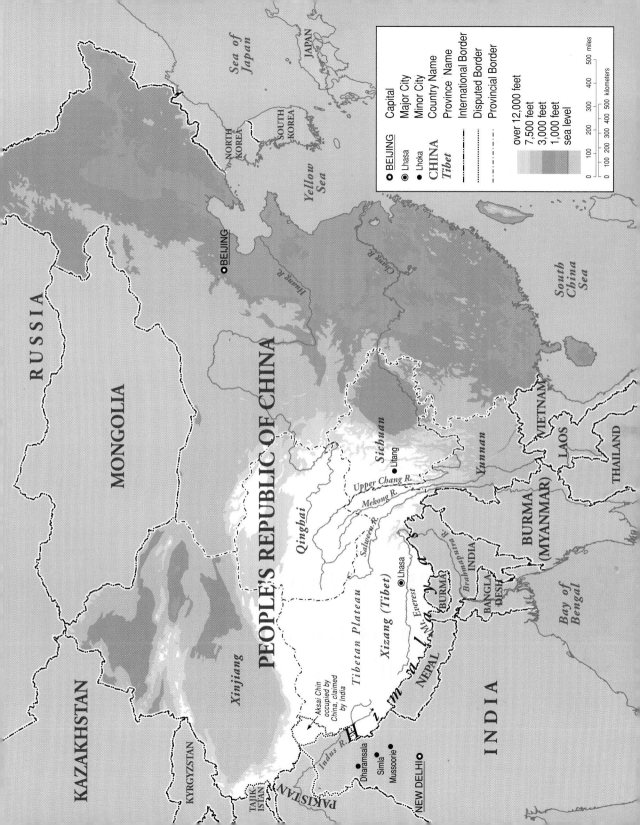

RUSSIA

Sea of Japan

JAPAN

NORTH KOREA

SOUTH KOREA

Yellow Sea

MONGOLIA

BEIJING

Huang R.

Chang R.

South China Sea

KAZAKHSTAN

PEOPLE'S REPUBLIC OF CHINA

Sichuan

Litang

Upper Chang R.

Mekong R.

Yunnan

VIETNAM

LAOS

THAILAND

Qinghai

Salween R.

BURMA (MYANMAR)

KYRGYZSTAN

Xinjiang

Tibetan Plateau

Xizang (Tibet)

Lhasa

Everest

Brahmaputra R.

INDIA

BURMA

BANGLA DESH

Bay of Bengal

Aksai Chin occupied by China, claimed by India

H i m a l a y a s

NEPAL

Indus R.

TAJIK ISTAN

PAKISTAN

Dharamsala
Simla
Mussoorie

NEW DELHI

INDIA

BEIJING — Capital
Lhasa — Major City
Lhoka — Minor City
CHINA — Country Name
Tibet — Province Name
International Border
Disputed Border
Provincial Border

over 12,000 feet
7,500 feet
3,000 feet
1,000 feet
sea level

500 miles
100 200 300 400 500 kilometers
0 100 200 300 400 500 miles

The PRC also imposed new taxes on land, cattle, houses, and other property. And, perhaps most important to Tibetans, China began to close monasteries and place restrictions on religious worship.

Tibetan leaders believed China's new policies violated Tibetan human rights. Tibetans responded with armed insurrections, mass protests, demonstrations, and individual acts of **civil disobedience.** China in turn cracked down harder on **dissidents**, restricting freedom of speech and outlawing Tibetan religious and cultural practices.

Cultural clashes between the Chinese and the Tibetans have fueled nearly 50 years of bitter conflict. And there's no end in sight. China maintains that Tibet has always been part of China. Tibet argues that it was independent before the PRC invaded in 1950. Until both sides can come to the table ready to really negotiate and compromise, the violence will continue.

THE LAND

The Tibet Autonomous Region (TAR), as Tibet is officially known, is situated in the southwestern part of China. The TAR shares its northern border with two Chinese provinces—the Xinjiang Uygur Autonomous Region and Qinghai. In the south, Tibet flanks the countries of Burma, India, Bhutan, and Nepal. Tibet borders India in the west and the Chinese provinces of Sichuan and Yunnan in the east. The total land area of the TAR is more than 470,000 square miles, or roughly the size of Texas, New Mexico, and Utah combined.

© Lin Jinghua/ChinaStock

Tibet's elevation—averaging more than 16,000 feet above sea level—makes it the most elevated populated region on earth. Obstacles such as Mount Everest (left), the highest mountain in the world, have contributed to Tibet's isolation and to the development of its unique history, culture, and economy.

A Difference of Opinion

Since the takeover, the Chinese have contended that Tibet rightfully belongs to China and that China controlled Tibet for centuries before 1950 when, the Chinese say, they simply reclaimed a historical territory.

Tibetan scholars, on the other hand, consider this version of history to be false. While acknowledging that China often provided military aid and protection throughout Tibet's history, Tibetans insist that they never traded Tibet's independence for Chinese protection or support. Tibetans argue that China's occupation of Tibet violates international law and oppresses the Tibetan people.

The most striking features of Tibet's geography are its mountain ranges. The dramatic Himalayas, home to Mount Everest (29,028 feet), are located along Tibet's southern frontier. Other important mountain systems include the Karakorum range in the southwest and the Kunlun in the north. Running parallel and due north from the main Himalayan chain are the Kailas Mountains, which average about 24,000 feet above sea level. Between these two Himalayan chains lies the Brahmaputra River, which flows from west to east through most of this region. The eastern part of Tibet features several large mountain chains and many deep river valleys. All of Asia's most important rivers—including the Brahmaputra, the Indus, the Mekong, the Salween, and the Chang (or Yangtze)—either originate in Tibet or flow through it.

The high, cold Tibetan Plateau dominates Tibet's interior and has an average elevation of about 15,000 feet. Running across Tibet from east to west, the plateau is the geographic "dividing line" that separates what is considered northern Asia from southern Asia.

In the river valleys of southern Tibet, where most of Tibet's people live, the climate is much milder. The south's lower elevation (about 12,000 feet) allows subsistence farmers to grow barley, Tibet's most important agricultural crop, and to raise livestock such as sheep and goats. Tibet's river valleys also support several rare animal species, including snow leopards, tigers, pandas, and wild horses.

LHASA

Lhasa, Tibet's most important city, is located in south central river valleys between the Himalayan and Trans-Himalayan mountain systems. With a population of more than 200,000, Lhasa, the capital of the TAR, is the region's economic and political hub. In the Tibetan language, the name means "God's City." Travelers and explorers from western Europe long considered Lhasa mysterious and exotic. Before the Chinese takeover, the capital was home to the Dalai Lama, Tibet's spiritual leader, who lived in Lhasa's Potala Palace. Because Lhasa was the holiest city in Tibet and the center of Tibetan religious, cultural, and spiritual life, outsiders were not allowed to visit. During this time Lhasa became known as the "Forbidden City."

THE PEOPLE OF TIBET

Most ethnic Tibetans are farmers who live in small,

Lush, terraced fields like elsewhere in China line Tibet's river valleys, such as the Khamba La pass (above).

adherence to the principles of Tibetan Buddhism, the religion practiced by 95 percent of all Tibetans. The main tenets of Tibetan Buddhism—reincarnation and attaining salvation by helping others—are similar to those held by Buddhists worldwide. The distinguishing feature of Tibetan Buddhists is their belief in the existence of living saints who are reincarnations of past saints, scholars, and deities. There-

isolated villages in the southern part of Tibet. Tibetan sheep and goat herders roam throughout the northern parts of Tibet. Tibetan traders in these and other rural areas buy manufactured goods from Nepal, India, or Burma and sell them along rural trade routes to the inhabitants of Tibet's many small towns and villages.

The most defining trait of the Tibetan people is their

A New Province

In 1965 China organized Tibet into a new province, the present-day TAR. Continuing debate over Tibet's boundaries fuels the Tibetan-Chinese conflict. When the Chinese speak of Tibet, they mean political Tibet—the TAR. When most Tibetans speak of Tibet, they mean historical Tibet, or what some scholars call ethnographic Tibet, an area that includes regions to the north and east of the TAR that are inhabited mostly by ethnic Tibetans.

These young shepherds herd sheep and goats near Gyantse. Rural Tibetans live in much the same way as their ancestors did.

The Chinese in Tibet

The Chinese living in Tibet have better educational opportunities, brighter job prospects, and higher living standards than Tibetans. Because of government wage incentives and the shortage of skilled labor in Tibet, Chinese immigrants can earn 10 times what they would make in other parts of China. In addition to those who work in mining or forestry, many Chinese immigrants have started businesses in Tibet to serve the growing Chinese population. In 1992 Tibetans owned only about 300 of more than 12,000 shops, businesses, and restaurants in Lhasa.

Many Chinese have moved to Tibet and opened their own businesses and restaurants, like the one at right.

fore, Tibetan Buddhist monks and nuns are much more than religious figureheads or symbols. They represent a system of leadership and authority that is strongly rooted in Tibetan culture and history. Before the Chinese takeover, Tibet's religious leaders also controlled the government.

Ethnic Chinese, called Han, have arrived in large numbers since 1950. By offering generous wage incentives and bonuses, China has encouraged Chinese citizens to move to Tibet and to take jobs in the construction, mining, and timber industries. Chinese entrepreneurs, many from the province of Sichuan, have flocked to

Tibet to establish profitable businesses that cater to the new arrivals. Many of these Chinese immigrants hope to make a better life for themselves and their families in Tibet, where they enjoy greater economic opportunities than they do in other Chinese provinces. In addition to the financial incentives, some young people come seeking adventure or the chance to fulfill what they see as their patriotic duty to help build the economy in an underdeveloped part of China.

While most Chinese have settled in Lhasa and the smaller surrounding towns in south central Tibet, a growing number are going to rural

parts of southeastern Tibet, especially to areas where mining operations have expanded. Beginning in 1992, the government has also encouraged Chinese immigrants to settle in agricultural areas of Tibet. Still, Tibetans vastly outnumber Chinese in the least economically developed parts of Tibet.

ECONOMY

Xizang, the Chinese word for Tibet, translates into "western treasure house." It's an accurate description because

Tibet contains extensive deposits of uranium, borax, lithium, copper, and chromite. In fact, Tibet has about half the world's supply of lithium, used in batteries and for chemical synthesis. China has aggressively tapped Tibet's natural resources, mining the region's mineral wealth and harvesting old growth forests in southeastern Tibet. Tibet's powerful rivers represent a huge potential source of hydroelectric power. China has begun to construct dams to harness this energy.

China has sought to foster economic growth by pouring money into the TAR. In the 1980s, China invested more money per capita in Tibet—an average of nearly $200 million per year—than it sent to any other region of China. In 1996 alone, China invested the equivalent of $600 million—about two-thirds of Tibet's total economy that year—into the region. In the 1990s, China sought to expand Tibet's economy by focusing on what it called the "pillar industries"—mining, forestry,

tourism, and construction. At the same time, China began to encourage Tibetans to get involved more in private enterprise.

Tourism is one of Tibet's fastest-growing industries, attracting people who seek mountaineering expeditions, religious pilgrimages, and adventure trips. The Chinese have invested in Tibet's **infrastructure** to make the region more accessible and have spent millions to restore some of Tibet's historic monasteries, including the Potala Palace in Lhasa.

Chinese investment in the region has been somewhat successful. In both 1995 and 1996, for example, Tibet's economy grew by more than 10 percent, outpacing growth in China. Yet Tibet and its people remain highly dependent on Chinese investments. If the Chinese government were to withdraw economic resources from the TAR, the people of Tibet would face a bleak economic picture. Tibet has not yet developed a strong economic base that could raise the standard of living, especially for Tibetans.

While China has made major economic investments in

© Dennis Cox/ChinaStock

Buddhist pilgrims prostrate themselves in front of the Jokhang Temple, bowing and sliding forward repeatedly throughout the day to show their devotion to Buddha.

> *The Chinese central government will welcome the Dalai Lama to return to the motherland so long as he gives up his advocacy of Tibetan independence and admits that Tibet is an integrated part of China.*
>
> —Gyaltsen Norbu, chair of the Tibet Autonomous Region

Tibet's economy, the income gap between the region's two major **ethnic groups** is growing. Tibet's Chinese population has gained the most from China's development of natural resources in the region. More than 90 percent of jobs created in the mining and forestry industries have gone to Chinese immigrants or temporary workers. Almost all of the minerals, lumber, and other resources extracted from Tibet's soil and forests are shipped to China.

LOOKING AHEAD

The outlook for a peaceful resolution of the ongoing conflict between the Chinese and Tibetans is uncertain. During the 1980s and 1990s, the Dalai Lama put forth a number of proposals for future Tibet-China arrangements that do not require Tibetan independence.

But the Chinese government, busy dealing with economic unrest in other parts of China, has largely ignored these gestures. The government continues to assert that the Dalai Lama's efforts are a trick to build support for the Tibetan independence movement. Given the wide difference of opinion on Tibet's proper status within the PRC, it is unlikely that conflict on the "Roof of the World" will be resolved anytime soon. ⊕

Toying with Nature

China's use of Tibet's natural resources has stirred great controversy. Environmental scientists are concerned about the link between deforestation, overgrazing, and mining in Tibet and the highly destructive flooding of Asia's seven major rivers. During the past decade alone, flooding has caused more than $500 million in damage and has killed thousands of people. Scientists are also concerned that damage to Tibet's forests may affect the weather and climate in Asia and, in turn, alter global weather patterns elsewhere in the world.

Chinese logging companies cut down Tibet's forests and ship the logs to other provinces. These logs made their way to Chengdu in Sichuan province.

MAJOR PLAYERS IN THE CONFLICT

Dalai Lama

Panchen Lama

The Fourteenth Dalai Lama Religious and political leader of Tibet and Tibetan Buddhists worldwide. He served as the ruler of Tibet from 1940 to 1959, when he fled to India after the invasion of Chinese troops. The Dalai Lama resides in Dharamsala, India, and remains an advocate for Tibet's independence.

The Eleventh Panchen Lama Religious and political leader of Tibet, second in stature to the Dalai Lama. The Eleventh Panchen Lama was chosen in 1995 by the Chinese government, a decision that went against the Dalai Lama's own choice and led to more controversy between Tibetans and the Chinese government.

People's Liberation Army (PLA) Formerly known as the Red Army, the PLA formed in the 1930s under the leadership of communist leader Mao Zedong. The PLA launched a full-scale military assault on Tibet in 1950, enforcing communist practices on the province.

People's Republic of China (PRC) In 1949 the Chinese Communist Party (CCP) gained control of China, creating the PRC. The Chinese lifestyle is made up of communist ideology, Buddhist and Taoist beliefs, and "modern" business practices that have been encouraged by the country's opening to foreign ideas.

Tibet Autonomous Region (TAR) A province of the People's Republic of China that maintains it has been made a part of the PRC unwillingly. The Tibetans' traditional culture remains in its rural and mountainous regions, while its cities are filled with Chinese cultural, economic, and architectural influences.

People's Liberation Army

Tibet Information Network and Human Rights Watch A watchdog group that issued a 1996 report detailing the political dissident arrests, torture of prisoners, and popular discontent in Tibet. The group found increased incidents of human rights violations occurring between 1994 and 1996.

People's Republic of China

Union of India Since 1947, when India gained its independence from Britain, the country has sometimes sided with the Chinese and at other times backed Tibetans. The Dalai Lama has lived there since 1959. In recent years, Indian diplomats have worked with China and Tibet to negotiate an end to the conflict.

Frank R. Wolf, U.S. Representative A Republican congressman from Virginia, Wolf visited Tibet in 1997 to observe human rights conditions. Following his visit, Wolf castigated the Chinese for destroying Tibetan culture, persecuting religious followers, and attempting to replace Tibetan culture by encouraging large numbers of Chinese to immigrate to Tibet. The Chinese government responded by accusing Wolf of trying to undermine ties between the United States and China.

National Flag of Tibet

Wu Jinghua Appointed the head of the Tibetan Communist Party by the Chinese in 1985. A member of the Yi ethnic group, Wu appeared in Tibetan dress at religious ceremonies and donated money to monks. Under his leadership, the streets of Lhasa were renamed using their traditional Tibetan names. Wu encouraged his officers to learn the Tibetan language. In the early 1990s, Wu was replaced by reformer Hu Jintao.

Union of India

1

THE RECENT CONFLICT AND ITS EFFECTS

In recent years, people around the world have paid more attention to the conflict in Tibet. Films—such as *Seven Years in Tibet* (1997), the story of an Austrian mountain climber's experience and his friendship with the Dalai Lama, and *Kundun* (1997), a depiction of the early life and times of the Dalai Lama—have heightened interest in the conflict. Through these and other movies and books, millions have learned more about Tibet and its stormy relationship with China.

A REFLECTION OF REAL LIFE

As movie audiences have watched the drama of Tibet on the silver screen, they could also follow news accounts of related real-life events. In September 1997, for example, a group of about 200 Tibetan **refugees** living in New Delhi, India,

Kundun *recounted the Fourteenth Dalai Lama's early life story and his initial dealings with the Chinese government.*

© Mario Tursi/The Everett Collection

marched through the city's streets to protest the continued imprisonment of Tanak Jigme Sangpo, the longest-held political prisoner in Tibet. Clad in colorful traditional Tibetan garments, the protesters carried banners as they marched to the Chinese embassy. After they arrived, Tibetans submitted a statement pleading with the Chinese government to release Sangpo.

Tanak Jigme Sangpo was a schoolteacher at the Lhasa Primary School before he was arrested in 1960 for expressing pro-independence views. He was officially tried and found guilty of "corrupting the minds of schoolchildren" because he taught his students about Tibetan culture and history. Since his arrest, he has been in prison and has spent many years in solitary confinement.

HUMAN RIGHTS CONCERNS

Aside from his lengthy prison term, Tanak Jigme Sangpo's story is not unusual. Tibetans who challenge China's authority are routinely ar-

Seven Years in Tibet *details the exchange of ideas between the Dalai Lama and author Heinrich Harrer.*

the Chinese government. Some survive punishments such as torture, beatings, starvation diets, and forced marches, but many die in prison or simply are never heard from again.

In recent years, many groups—including the United Nations and human rights advocacy organizations around the world—have accused the Chinese of violating Tibetans' human rights. According to these groups, the Chinese unlawfully arrest, detain, and torture Tibetans who protest the Chinese occupation of Tibet; deliberately destroy Tibet's unique culture and civilization; and discriminate against Tibetans.

Most outside observers believe that in the 1990s the Chinese have only stepped

rested, detained, and, in many cases, tortured for "advancing the cause of **separatism.**" Groups such as the Tibet Information Network of London and Human Rights Watch/Asia of New York estimate that at any one time the Chinese hold more than 3,000 Tibetans as prisoners of conscience.

Under Chinese law, these political prisoners have no lawyers, and they aren't granted the right to a fair trial. Their only hope for freedom lies in renouncing

their support for Tibetan independence and in giving police the names of friends and family members who oppose

Does Nonviolence Work?

Although most Tibetans feel bound by their religion to protest injustice through nonviolent means, some young people are increasingly frustrated with this approach and are willing to use violence to oppose China's policies. In fact, Tibet has become China's most rebellious and least stable territory. Protests by Tibetans, Tibetans' religious beliefs, and support for Tibetan human rights are all factors that undermine Chinese rule. The Chinese government cites this instability as a reason for granting Tibet less autonomy than any other region in China.

Refugee Crisis

Thousands of Tibetans have left, finding freedom in India. Experts estimate that between 120,000 and 125,000 Tibetan refugees live in India.

The road to freedom is dangerous. Refugees must climb through the remote and steep mountains. Most take the trip during the winter months, when Tibet's international borders are less likely to be carefully guarded.

Some are caught while trying to escape into neighboring Nepal and Bhutan. The Chinese often reward police and border guards with cash for each Tibetan they capture and return to Tibet. The Chinese arrest and torture many of these refugees. Others die of starvation, hypothermia, or disease before reaching safety and freedom.

Although the largest Tibetan refugee population is in Dharamsala, India, Tibetan refugees have also settled in Switzerland, Nepal, Bhutan, Australia, Germany, and the United States. In 1991 the United States allowed 1,000 Tibetan refugees, chosen by a lottery system, to cross its borders. These refugees are now settled in 34 states and more than 100 communities across the country.

Tenzin Tsepak, a Tibetan refugee who lives in Minneapolis, Minnesota, escaped Tibet when he was 13 years old. His parents and brothers were arrested and killed in Tibet for resisting Chinese authority before he was six. At age six, he was alone and forced to fend for himself. To earn money for food, he worked as a shepherd in a remote border region of Tibet. Like many young Tibetans, he had no opportunity to attend school.

Some Tibetans choose to leave Tibet for greater freedom elsewhere. Many Tibetan refugees, such as the woman above, flee to and remain in India. Many Tibetans have also emigrated to the United States.

Eventually, Tenzin Tsepak and a friend decided to escape. They found their path to freedom through the mountains between Tibet and Bhutan. Yet the journey was much more difficult than he or his friend could have ever imagined. Bhutanese police arrested the two boys at the border, charged them with being Chinese spies, and threw them in jail for two years. They were eventually deported to India, where they spent several years living in refugee camps.

In India Tenzin Tsepak attended the Tibetan Home School in Dharamsala and met the Dalai Lama. After finishing school, Tenzin went to work for the Dalai Lama's government. In 1991 he came to the United States along with 1,000 other Tibetan refugees who were granted asylum. Despite many hardships along the way, his struggle for freedom was worth it. "In Tibet, we don't have any freedom," Tenzin said. "You can't do what you want or go where you want."

up political and religious repression in Tibet. The Tibet Information Network and Human Rights Watch issued a report in 1996 stating that political dissident arrests, torture in prisons, and popular discontent in Tibet have all increased since 1994.

Numerous sources have supported the report's observations about Chinese repression in Tibet. Recently, for example, reporters with the *Philadelphia Inquirer* interviewed a number of Tibetan refugees for a series of articles on life in Tibet. The stories included graphic descriptions of what happens to Tibetans who challenge Chinese authority.

One article described the case of a teenager who was arrested for participating in a Free Tibet rally. Although she was imprisoned for more than two years, her Chinese captors never formally charged her with a crime. Chinese police regularly beat and tortured her until she revealed names of friends and family members who shared her views. Other Tibetans interviewed for the *Inquirer* shared similar stories. And an independent physician who examined each victim found physical evidence to confirm their accounts.

U.S. Representative Frank R. Wolf, a Republican congressman from Virginia, traveled to Tibet in August 1997 to observe human rights conditions firsthand. At a news conference following his visit, Wolf accused the Chinese of destroying Tibetan culture, persecuting religious followers, and seeking to overwhelm Tibetan culture by encouraging massive Chinese immigration to Tibet.

Chinese government officials responded by accusing Congressman Wolf of lying about conditions in Tibet and of attempting to use the Tibetan situation to weaken ties between the United States and China. They insisted that China's policies have improved life in Tibet by boosting the TAR's economy and by increasing the Tibetan life expectancy from 35 to 65 years through improved health care. Government officials continue to deny the charge that China is set on eradicating Tibetan culture, noting that China has spent $36 million since the 1980s to renovate many damaged or decaying monasteries.

THROUGH TIBETAN EYES

The Tibetan government-in-exile claims that the PRC restricts cultural, religious, and political expression in Tibet. For example, since the riots of the late 1980s, the PRC has restricted Tibetan's rights

Refugees for Freedom

It's not surprising that Tibetan refugees are among the most ardent advocates of Tibetan independence. In January 1999, for example, a group of about 60 Tibetan refugees in India completed a 250-kilometer (155-mile) peace march to urge the United Nations to reopen talks on Tibetan independence. The protesters, members of the Tibet Youth Congress, concluded their march at the Chinese embassy in New Delhi, the capital of India, where they chanted "Freedom for Tibet" and "Down with China." The group stormed the embassy gates and about 20 people scaled the walls and joined in burning two Chinese flags to protest China's control of Tibet.

This old Tibetan currency (above) *is proof to some Tibetans that their province was once an independent country. Lhasa* (below) *is a city of duality. Tibetan pilgrims bustle along busy streets toward the ancient Jokhang Temple while huge Chinese-built hotels loom behind them.*

to gather for public meetings or to discuss the status of Tibet, the presence of Chinese immigrants in Tibet, or the possible return of the Dalai Lama. Through such policies, many believe that China has managed to weaken Tibet's cultural and religious practices and institutions. The Chinese argue that they are only helping to upgrade Tibet and to bring its people into modern times.

Since the PRC invaded Tibet in 1950, China has pulled down many historic buildings and monasteries and has auctioned off or destroyed cultural artifacts. Discos, restaurants, houses, and shops with a distinctively Chinese architectural style often fill the vacant lots. The Chinese have announced that they intend to leave only a few major tourist attractions standing in Lhasa, such as the Potala Palace and the Jokhang Temple.

Chinese authorities have also placed restrictions on religious worship in Tibet. It is against the law to possess, display, or distribute pictures of the Dalai Lama. The Chinese government forbids Tibetan scholars and historians at the University of Tibet in Lhasa from offering lectures on **Buddhism** to their classes. The Chinese have banned books and plays on Tibetan history. In addition, the Chinese government condemned resistance to Chinese authority and ordered Tibetan writers to reflect working-class views in their work.

In the spring of 1997, the government established political re-education teams in Tibet's monasteries. The teams instructed monks to sign written statements denouncing their spiritual leader, the Dalai Lama. Those who refused to obey were locked in their monasteries for weeks. The Chinese government has also set up work brigades to monitor activities within all monas-

teries. Monks and nuns can only participate in approved displays of religious practice such as those put on for the benefit of tourists.

THE CHINESE POINT OF VIEW

The PRC maintains that its primary goal in Tibet is to modernize and develop the region's economy. Any action that the Chinese government takes is to help them attain industrialization. For example, government-sponsored economic programs in Tibet have attracted Han Chinese immigrants to the region. Tibetans protested the massive influx of Chinese, accusing the Chinese government of attempting to **sinicize** Tibet. The PRC argues that it never intended to sinicize Tibet—only to modernize it. In 1984 the PRC heeded Tibetan

protests and placed a ban on Chinese immigration to Tibet. The ban didn't last long, however. When development projects lacked skilled labor to complete jobs, the PRC again allowed Chinese immigrants to settle in the region.

Tibetans also object to the many new Chinese buildings and businesses that have cropped up in Lhasa and other cities. The PRC asserts that the influx of Han Chinese workers to fill jobs created by economic development has generated the need for Chinese restaurants, shops, and other businesses in Tibet.

To the Chinese, historic Tibetan culture, including religious isolation, is an obstacle to the continued social, economic, and political development of Tibet. The PRC's position on freedom of religion in Tibet has evolved over the years. In the 1970s and early 1980s, China loosened its grip on Tibetan religious affairs, allowing Tibetans to reopen some monasteries and to perform religious ceremonies again. The riots that erupted in the late 1980s forced the PRC to rethink its approach.

Why Such a Threat?

It wasn't long before religion became a source of heated debate between the two cultures. For Tibetans, religion was simply part of life. Before the PRC takeover, many young Tibetans—usually at least one child per family—entered monasteries to devote their lives to religious study. This religious devotion posed problems for the PRC. Because Buddhism held such a prominent position in Tibetan life, PRC leaders believed that the religion detracted from their ability to govern and to maintain control over the Tibetan population.

The riots threatened China's control over the region, which in turn affected Tibet's economic development. In the early 1990s, the Chinese government decided to reinstate the religious restrictions it had lifted more than a decade earlier. To maintain its authority, the PRC worked to prevent riots by putting more soldiers on the streets and installing closed-circuit video surveillance cameras to keep a close watch on potential troublemakers. The cameras monitor activities in the Tibetan quarter of Lhasa, the busy marketplaces near the Jokhang Temple, and the altar rooms in the Potala Palace.

The Chinese government defends its right to deal with Tibetan separatists and those who engage in religious observances not authorized by the Communist Party. Sometimes such observances include worship services, rituals, and ceremonies that are central to the practice of Tibetan Buddhism. Although the government claims that monks and nuns can worship freely, China also accuses the Dalai Lama and his supporters of stirring up trouble in Tibet by "using religion as a cover for the Tibetan independence movement."

Years of failed attempts to negotiate with the Dalai Lama and his advisers have fueled mistrust between the PRC and the Tibetan government-in-exile. The Chinese believe that they have given the Dalai Lama plenty of opportunities to settle the Tibetan conflict and to still preserve his dignity. They claim that the Dalai Lama has replied to PRC negotiation attempts with unrealistic demands one too many times. These experiences have led the PRC to conclude that the Dalai Lama is not interested in settling the conflict. The Chinese government claims that the

Different Worlds

It's not surprising that the People's Republic of China (PRC) doesn't see eye-to-eye with the Dalai Lama. The two sides come from completely different worlds of thought.

The communist regime is led by members of the Chinese Communist Party (CCP). In China, the CCP decides what children will study in school, what may or may not be printed in newspapers or aired on television, and where citizens may live and work.

Buddhism has been the foundation on which Tibetans have built their culture. Monasteries, where monks and nuns live and study, are centers for religion, medicine, art, and culture. Religion holds so much clout in Tibet that the Dalai Lama is the region's spiritual and political leader.

Because of the depth of Buddhist influence in Tibetan culture, Chinese government policies hit the Tibetans more forcefully than they did their Chinese counterparts. Communist theory generally discourages religious worship and the Communist Party views religion as a threat to communism, so Tibetan culture fell under direct attack. Since the late 1970s, the PRC government has relaxed some of its antireligious stances. But it still feels threatened by and tries to control religious organizations.

The PRC flag flies high, across the street from the Potala Palace in Lhasa.

Dalai Lama stirs up the emotions of the Tibetan people and keeps alive hopes of an independent Tibet. In response to this, the PRC has officially banned photos of the Dalai Lama in Tibet and forbidden talk of his return to Lhasa.

Meanwhile, neither side shows signs of working toward a peaceful resolution to the conflict any time soon.

At the heart of the dispute is who controls what territory. The PRC is unwilling to grant Tibet limited autonomy, for fear that Tibetans will continue to fight for total independence. The Tibetan government-in-exile has given up on its original request for total independence and agreed to settle for having control over the region's religious affairs. But

the Dalai Lama holds fast to demands that parts of surrounding Chinese provinces that are mostly populated by ethnic Tibetans become a part of Tibet. China believes that this is asking too much. Until these issues are resolved—issues that have been the source of tension between the two nations for many, many years—the conflict will continue. ⊕

THE CONFLICT'S ROOTS

The pivotal event in Tibetan-Chinese relations—a royal wedding—took place more than 1,000 years ago. Long ago it was an established practice for the Chinese to send princesses to conquered kingdoms to introduce Chinese culture and civilization to the region. In the seventh century, Songtsen Gampo, considered the greatest king of what was called the Tibetan kingdom, married Princess Wengcheng of China. This historic union had important political consequences. In marrying Princess Wengcheng, Songtsen Gampo strengthened Tibet's growing empire and opened a new chapter in Tibetan-Chinese relations.

To understand more about the ongoing conflict between Tibet and China, it's necessary to step more than 1,500 years back in time. Historians know very little about the people who lived in Tibet before the sixth century. Research indicates that many distinct groups or tribes, each headed by its own chief, made up the Tibetan peoples. These nomadic tribes traveled from place to place in search of food and trading opportunities. During the sixth century, some of these Tibetan chiefs united behind a single leader, and eventually the Tibetans emerged as a distinct people. The first known references to the people of Tibet are found in Chinese historical records, which describe Tibetan attacks along China's borders.

Under Songtsen Gampo, Tibet grew more powerful and influential. Known as a strong military and political leader, Songtsen Gampo built a powerful army that seized Chinese territory along China's western borders. He also introduced the Tibetan people to the writ-

Folktales and Legends

According to Tibetan folktales and legends, the first Tibetan was produced by the mating of a monkey and a she-devil. The colorful fable is a prime example of the similarities and distinct differences between Tibetan and Chinese culture. To the Tibetans, the monkey is a sacred animal with an honored place in religious folklore. Monkey gods also frequently appear in Chinese legends. Yet the Chinese also use images of the hairy monkey to insult people and cultures that they consider inferior. Although it's only a legend, the Chinese look with contempt on Tibetans' claims to be descended from the monkey.

Royal Wedding

Chinese young people are expected to extract two lessons from the royal wedding story—that Tibet's destiny has always been linked to China's and that Tibetan culture has long been inferior to Chinese traditions. Yet most historians—certainly most Tibetans—have a different view. Tibetan scholars believe that after Songtsen Gampo's troops seized territory in western China, he demanded the princess's hand in marriage. The Chinese emperor's consent was a peace offering to the Tibetans. The story of this royal wedding and its controversial interpretations highlight the differences between Tibetan and Chinese historical viewpoints. These conflicting versions of the past remain woven throughout the current conflict.

Songtsen Gampo (above), *king of Tibet in the 600s, and Princess Wengcheng* (right), *princess of China and wife of Songtsen Gampo*

ten Tibetan language and to the Buddhist religion.

Between A.D. 630 and 800, Buddhism spread throughout Tibet, forever changing the region's culture, economy, and society. By the 790s, Buddhism played a central role in Tibetan society. The religion had absorbed or replaced many of the important elements of the early religions practiced by Tibetan tribespeople. As Tibetans embraced Buddhism, many trained to become Buddhist priests and built monasteries to promote further study.

WAR AND PEACE WITH CHINA

During Songtsen Gampo's reign and for at least two centuries thereafter, Tibet was a constant thorn in China's side. Tibetan armies seized land from the Chinese, vastly expanding Tibetan territory. For a while the Chinese were able to contain Tibetan expansion by paying tribute to the tune of 50,000 rolls of silk to the Tibetan kings each year. (Silk was a highly prized and profitable product.) Tibetan rulers penalized Chinese

Tibetan Buddhists light yak butter lamps and chant during their devotions to Buddha.

Tibetan Buddhism

Buddhists believe that, after death, people experience a series of reincarnations, or rebirths. They continue to be reincarnated, or reborn, until they have performed a certain number of good deeds. At this point, a Buddhist believer reaches a state of heavenly contentment called Nirvana. A person can also choose to trade the experience of Nirvana to become a *bodhisattva*. As a bodhisattva, one can return to earth in human form to help others attain Nirvana. The Dalai Lama is considered to be the reincarnation of the bodhisattva Chenrezig, the patron deity of Tibet.

Like other religions, Tibetan Buddhism has come to be divided into different sects. Over time, the Gelugpa sect, developed in the fifteenth century by Tsong Khapa, became the most powerful group within Tibetan Buddhism. Monks in the Gelugpa sect wore yellow hats and emphasized the importance of monastic discipline in their religious practice. The sect's highest-ranking priest, the Dalai Lama, or "God King," became the recognized head of Tibetan Buddhism and the leader of the Tibetan government. The second-highest-ranking priest in the Gelugpa sect is the Panchen Lama. The Dalai Lama is thought to be the incarnation of Buddha's body, while the Panchen Lama is the incarnation of Buddha's mind.

emperors who failed to pay these annual fees. For instance, in 763 a new Chinese emperor failed to pay the silk tribute, and the Tibetans retaliated, capturing an important region of China and replacing the Chinese emperor with a puppet ruler who was favored by the Tibetan king.

During the ninth and tenth centuries, most historians believe that Tibet and China regarded one another as equals. In 821 Tibet and China signed the so-called "Treaty of Uncle and Nephew," the first of many peace treaties. This important agreement between the two countries was recorded in both Tibetan and Chinese on a stone pillar that still stands in Lhasa.

Despite the rise of the Tibetan kingdom, internal divisions threatened its stability. Tibet's unity depended on strong leadership, but as the empire expanded, kings found it increasingly difficult to control their military leaders in far-flung border regions. Religious oppression had also divided Tibetans into rival camps. Although Songtsen Gampo had brought Buddhism to Tibet, his descendants actually

> *Now that the two countries have been allied by this great treaty, it is necessary that messengers should once again be sent by the old route to maintain communications and carry the exchange of friendly messages regarding the harmonious relations between the Uncle and the Nephew.*
>
> —From the Treaty of Uncle and Nephew

persecuted followers of the Buddhist religion.

Eventually, a split in Tibet's royal family broke the kingdom into warring factions. When Tibetan king Langdarma, the last descendant of Songtsen Gampo, died in 842, the once-powerful Tibetan kingdom began to fall apart. By 905 China's Tang Dynasty, which had outlived the Tibetan kingdom, fell into decline as well. As a result, Tibet and China each became quite isolated.

For the next two centuries, various Tibetan nobles established separate princedoms in Tibet and in western China. Scholars know little about this period of Tibetan history. Other than occasional border skirmishes between rival tribes, there was little or no contact between China and Tibet.

UP FROM THE ASHES

Around 1042 Tibet experienced a period of renewal. During this time, a great Buddhist teacher from India named Pandit Atisha arrived. His followers established powerful and wealthy monasteries that became control centers for Buddhist monks who ruled Tibetan secular life for nearly a thousand years. Following the Buddhist revival, life in the Tibetan kingdom remained peaceful and stable for several centuries.

In the thirteenth century, Ghengis Khan, a Mongol

Tibetan Feudalism

Under Tibet's historic feudal economic system, the majority of Tibetans were poor and repressed. For the most part, powerful religious elite and secular noble families owned and controlled the bulk of Tibet's agriculturally productive land and wielded all of the power in Tibetan religious and political institutions. Some members of the nobility abused their privileged positions by extracting bribes for favorable treatment, seizing peasant crops, and forcing peasant women to serve as their "temporary brides."

Most Tibetans belonged to the class of peasants or serfs. Some spent their lives as slaves to aristocratic families. They farmed the land and harvested the crops. Under this feudal system, the peasants turned over their harvest to the wealthy landlords. In exchange, they were given a measure of the harvest, which they used to feed their families. Serfs had little or no opportunity to improve their status in Tibetan society.

When the PLA went to Tibet to recruit new members into their ranks, they had no problem finding plenty of Tibetan cadres among the society's lower class—those who had been miserable under Tibet's old system.

warlord, threatened this period of relative calm. Known for conquering and killing people, pillaging their property, and seizing their land, Ghengis Khan had become the most powerful ruler in Asia by 1207. As his Mongol Empire spread toward Tibet and China, leading Tibetan nobles feared that their land would be the next to fall. But Ghengis Khan died without invading or interfering in Tibet.

After his death, however, Ghengis Khan's grandson, Godan Khan, sought greater influence over Tibet. In 1240 Godan Khan and his troops invaded Tibet, killing many Tibetans and looting Tibetan property. Godan Khan's troops never reached Lhasa, however. A few years later, Godan Khan appointed Sakya Pandita, Tibet's most eminent lama or priest at the time, as vice regent of Tibet.

For the first time, political power in Tibet was placed in

The revered Fifth Dalai Lama became Tibet's leader when Mongolian Gusri Khan died in 1655.

the hands of Buddhist monks. While the Tibetan nobles did not fully accept the authority of the Mongol-backed Buddhist lamas, they had no choice but to submit to the power of the Mongol Empire.

The Chinese, subdued in 1279, hated their Mongol conquerors. In 1368 they overthrew the Mongols and established the Ming Dynasty. In Tibet the end of Mongol rule was much less dramatic. Tibet maintained diplomatic ties with the far-away Mongols, whose influence eventually faded in Tibet. Power remained in the hands of the Buddhist monks.

During the Ming dynasty, the Chinese exercised no authority over Tibet. A relationship did exist, and Tibetan monks often journeyed to China on tribute

> For the first time, political power in Tibet was placed in the hands of Buddhist monks. . . . [The Tibetan nobles] had no choice but to submit to the power of the Mongol Empire.

missions. For the next 200 years, Tibet and China developed along their own separate paths, with relatively little contact.

THE RELATIONSHIP CHANGES

In 1642 Tibetans invited Gusri Khan, a Mongol prince, to visit Tibet. Warmly welcomed by his Tibetan hosts, Gusri Khan appointed the Fifth Dalai Lama as the country's religious head. A man of remarkable intellect, stature, character, and achievement, "The Great Fifth" was a skilled leader and organizer who handled diplomatic affairs with ease. He is still regarded as one of Tibet's greatest Dalai Lamas.

Under Gusri Khan's influence, the Fifth Dalai Lama tried to establish a friendly relationship with China's ruling Qing dynasty, which had overthrown the Ming dynasty in 1645. The Dalai Lama embarked on a grand tour of China, during which Chinese leaders greeted him with the pomp and circumstance befitting an independent head of state. When Gusri Khan died in 1655, the Dalai Lama became Tibet's undisputed political and religious leader. Succeeding Dalai Lamas have continued to maintain this authority.

When the Fifth Dalai Lama died in 1682, Tibet's relationship with China again became more ambivalent. Sangye Gyatso, regent of Tibet who had long served the Fifth Dalai Lama as his top adviser, selected the next Dalai Lama. The Sixth Dalai Lama turned out to be

The Mongol Connection

The Chinese claim that Tibet has been under China's rule as far back as the fourteenth century, because the Mongols conquered Tibet after they had already conquered China. Since Tibet and China were both part of the Mongolian Empire, they argue, the two countries had essentially been united into one.

Yet most Tibetan, North American, and European scholars take a different view. While it is true that China and Tibet were linked for a time because both were conquered by the same foreign power—the Mongols—the two nations regained their independence separately. Also, after China had shaken off the Mongols, it did not immediately seek to regain control over former Mongol territory or to exercise any authority over Tibet. The two nations quickly went their separate ways after defeating the Mongols.

Corbis/Bettmann

Genghis Khan (above) *established the Mongol Empire by conquering China and Tibet and keeping Tibet under the Khan's power for about two centuries.*

CHAPTER 2   *The Conflict's Roots*

poorly suited to lead his people. More interested in drinking, socializing, and writing love songs, he refused to take the vows necessary to become a monk. Because the Sixth Dalai Lama had no interest in affairs of state, Sangye Gyatso ran the government. In the early 1700s, Sangye Gyatso forged a military alliance with Galdan Khan, a powerful Mongol leader who threatened China's interests in central Asia. The alliance infuriated the Chinese emperor Kang Xi, who urged Lhabsang Khan, king of Mongolia and ally to China, to invade Tibet. On reaching Lhasa in 1706, the Chinese-backed Mongol troops killed Sangye Gyatso and arrested the Sixth Dalai Lama.

Despite the Sixth Dalai Lama's shortcomings, Tibetans remained loyal to him and were bitterly angry when they discovered that he had died under mysterious circumstances while on the way to China. Emperor Kang Xi and King Lhabsang appointed a new Dalai Lama themselves, announcing that the Sixth Dalai Lama had not been chosen correctly. Tibetans ignored China's choice and instead—using their age-old process—gave the title to a baby in the holy city of Litang.

Soon after this gesture of Tibetan independence, China's emperor drafted the Edict of 1720. Inscribed in four languages on a stone pillar in Lhasa, the edict implied, but did not state openly, that China had held a special influence in Tibetan affairs since at least 1640. Some scholars have described the edict as Chinese **propaganda** because it creates the impression that China had greater authority over Tibet—and for a longer period of time—than is justified by historical evidence.

CHINA'S GROWING INFLUENCE

Initially the period that came to be known as the Chinese protectorate was a positive experience for Tibetans. On several occasions, China was able to restore peace, stability, and order in Tibet and to provide security against future invasions by the Mongols and other groups. For

Finding the Next Dalai Lama

During his lifetime, the Dalai Lama leaves clues as to where he thinks his reincarnation may appear. After his death, a select group of clergymen follows these suggestions, as well as any unusual phenomena, to search for the new Dalai Lama. There is an elaborate and ancient ritual for finding the next reincarnated Dalai Lama and for confirming the individual's status. Reincarnations may be found in a young child of either gender, although all the Dalai Lamas so far have been male. After the clergymen locate a youth, he must meet certain criteria. Distinguishing marks include large ears and moles located on the torso and beneath the arms. The moles indicate where arms could have been in a former life. If the youth meets all of the criteria, monks and lamas take the child from his home and immerse him in study. Citizens put the power of government and religious affairs into the Dalai Lama's control when he reaches the age of 18. Until then, a regent handles the Dalai Lama's responsibilities. The Dalai Lama himself leads a similar search for the new Panchen Lama.

the most part, China respected and preserved Tibet's traditional customs and government institutions.

China abolished the office of regent and replaced it with four ministers—all of whom were Tibetan aristocrats and former supporters of Lhabsang Kahn. The ministers were to advise the Dalai Lama on governmental affairs. When the Seventh Dalai Lama was too young to govern, an adviser or regent was assigned to make decisions for him. China granted the Tibetan government authority over land stretching from western Tibet to the reaches of the Upper Chang River. But power ultimately rested in the hands of the Chinese. A Chinese military governor commanding 2,000 troops had supreme authority over Tibet.

Tibetans initially welcomed China's presence, but before long they resented the larger country's military presence and regarded it as a burden. Sharp increases in prices and supply shortages always seemed to coincide with the appearance of Chinese troops in Lhasa. Tibetans also objected to the high taxes needed to main-tain the troops and began to call for their withdrawal. The Chinese emperor agreed in 1723. He stationed a civilian adviser in Lhasa to replace Tibet's military governor and pulled the troops out of Tibet.

Meanwhile, dissension among the four ruling ministers erupted in civil war in 1727. Some of the ministers assassinated Khangchennas, the chairman of the ministry, and tried to kill Pholhanas, one of his supporters. But Pholhanas escaped to south-western Tibet, where he gathered an army. Pholhanas's troops marched to Lhasa, where they defeated the remaining ministers and seized the city. Hearing of the coup attempt, China sent troops to maintain order. But by the time troops arrived two months later, Pholhanas had everything under control. Instead of sending the troops home, however, China's emperor ordered them to remain in Tibet. China feared that the Mongols, especially a subgroup called the Dzungars, would again interfere in Tibet. China reorganized Tibet's government and appointed two civil officers called **ambans** to represent China's interests in Tibet. Although ambans mainly were responsible for reporting to the emperor on Tibetan affairs, they also commanded a substantial military force.

At the same time, the Chinese emperor took action to ensure that the Tibetans not entertain any more ideas about revolt. He invited the Dalai Lama to Beijing, China's capital, to get him out of Lhasa. A Chinese escort led the Dalai Lama only as far as Litang, where he was to remain under indefinite watch. When the Dalai Lama returned to Lhasa seven years later, the Chinese ordered him to stay out of politics.

The Chinese began supporting the royal leadership of Phola Teji, one of Tibet's most effective political and military leaders. The Chinese emperor installed Phola Teji as king of Tibet, expecting him to govern Tibet in accordance with Chinese interests. Phola Teji followed China's plan for the most part and the Chinese trusted him. As a result, until his death in 1747, he was able to negotiate key issues and limit China's influence in Tibet.

Nevertheless, China still looked for ways to fortify its position in Tibet. The Chinese feared that, if left unchallenged, the Dalai Lama would use his religious influence to rally Tibetans against China. One way to reduce the Dalai Lama's power would be to create a rival religious authority of equal or nearly equal status. The Chinese looked for such a rival in the Panchen Lama—the second-highest-ranking priest in the Gelugpa sect of Tibetan Buddhism. To win the Panchen Lama's support, the Chinese promised to give him authority over vast areas of north central and western Tibet. But the Panchen Lama refused China's offer.

NEW THREATS TO STABILITY

Phola's younger son, Gyurmé Namgyal, succeeded his father as king of Tibet. Although the transition went smoothly, Tibet's relationship with China was soon threatened. Unlike Phola Teji, Gyurmé Namgyal fostered a strong dislike for foreign rule. Before long the new king of Tibet had convinced the emperor to reduce the number of troops stationed in Lhasa to 100

men. At the same time, Gyurmé Namgyal began plotting with the Dzungars, who still posed a threat to China.

Gyurmé Namgyal's plots eventually led to murder and his demise. Worried about possible competition from his male relatives, Gyurmé Namgyal arranged to have them killed. The ambans responded by inviting him to their residence and then murdering him. Although Gyurmé Namgyal was neither popular with the Dalai Lama nor with the Tibetan people, angry mobs took to the streets to protest foreign interference in Tibetan affairs. The Dalai Lama soon restored order, but the emperor sent troops to calm things anyway.

In 1750 the emperor's representatives again reorganized the Tibetan government, abolishing the Tibetan kingship and placing power in the hands of the Dalai Lama, or, more often than not, his regent until the Dalai Lama was old enough to rule. For the next 42 years, relations between Tibet and China were peaceful.

During the late 1780s, a group called the Gurkhas

twice invaded Tibet from their stronghold in Nepal. The Gurkhas followed the Hindu religion and viewed Tibetans and their Buddhist beliefs with contempt. Chinese troops repelled Gurkha troops both times, but the Chinese emperor was upset about the challenge to China's authority in Tibet. Ultimately, he decided to deter future aggression by tightening China's hold on Tibet.

Around 1793 China once again reorganized Tibet's government and asserted total control over Tibet's communications with the outside world. For example, the ambans had to approve all correspondence from the Dalai Lama and Panchen Lama to outsiders. To further isolate Tibet, China barred foreigners from visiting the region. The Chinese were particularly suspicious of the British, who had expanded their influence on the Indian subcontinent and who the Chinese suspected of helping the Gurkhas invade Tibet. In imposing these measures, China hoped to make it more difficult for foreign countries to forge relationships with Tibet. Such alliances, China felt, could threaten China's vital economic and military interests in Asia.

The Tibetans did not protest China's actions. They, too, were concerned about Britain's growing influence in the region, as well as that of British-backed Christian missionaries settling on the Indian-Chinese border. Nevertheless, Tibet continued to conduct at least some foreign relations with other countries.

PROBLEMS AT HOME

The 1800s were a time of internal turmoil for China. Rampant political corruption spurred a series of anti-imperial rebellions from 1796 to 1804. Although the government was able to end the rebellions, unrest remained strong.

Meanwhile, Britain's trade in opium, a drug grown on the British-controlled subcontinent, was affecting the Chinese economy. By 1839 China found itself at war with Britain over the opium trade. Chinese addicts used silver to pay for the drug, and, eventually, the amount of silver leaving China began to hurt the economy. By

The Panchen Lama's Role

Since 1728—when China's Manchu dynasty removed the Dalai Lama from power and tried to strengthen the Panchen Lama's influence in Tibet—a rivalry has existed between the two Tibetan leaders. China has enforced policies throughout history that have fueled the rivalry, at times offering large parcels of land, government posts, and even an army to the Panchen Lama. Although the Panchen Lama more often than not refused to accept these gifts, members of his entourage were known to be more willing to work with the Chinese. Whenever the Dalai Lama received word of a developing relationship between the Panchen Lama's constituents and the Chinese government, he became uneasy.

The Third Panchen Lama (1738–1780)—who was widely known to be a more effective leader than the Dalai Lama at the time—established ties with the British and the Chinese and set the precedent for future encounters with foreign powers. In 1903, for example, the Dalai Lama refused to talk to the British, but the Panchen Lama arranged a meeting with Sir Francis Younghusband, who invaded Tibet in 1904 and caused more than 300 Tibetan fatalities. When the British and the Chinese chose to negotiate with the Panchen Lama instead of with the Dalai Lama, the lama rivalry intensified. In 1910 the Panchen Lama fled Tibet and the Dalai Lama for China. Thereafter, the Chinese government made the Panchen Lama the center of a constant stream of plots to drive the two lamas further apart and to fuel mistrust between them.

1839 China and Britain were at war. China's defeat in 1842 expanded Britain's influence in Asia. But China's problems had just begun. Droughts, floods, and famine ravaged the countryside and affected millions of Chinese. When the government did

little to ease their suffering, villagers in southern China fought back in what became known as the Taiping Rebellion. Fighting raged from 1851 to 1864, killing as many as 30 million Chinese.

By the end of the 1800s, China's internal problems

weakened its power and influence in Tibet, as well as elsewhere in the region. After the Chinese-Japanese War in 1894, Japan seized part of Korea and all of Taiwan, areas that had seaports vital to the Chinese economy.

At the same time, European countries continued to take an active interest in Tibet. Tibet remained a closed society, but British, French, American, and Russian explorers all managed to enter the region. Competition among rival European empires that came to be known as the "Great Game"—especially the power struggle between Britain and Russia—drove much of this exploration.

During the 1880s and 1890s, Russia sought to de-

Britain and Tibet

The first official contact between Britain and Tibet occurred in 1772. An Indian leader had asked Britain to halt an invasion by neighboring Bhutan. The British were able to drive the Bhutanese back into Bhutan and, at the same time, to spark their first diplomatic exchange with Tibet. The Panchen Lama sent a cordial letter to Warren Hastings, the British leader, explaining that the Bhutanese people were subjects of the Dalai Lama and urging Britain not to invade Bhutan. Hastings assured him that Britain had no such plans but welcomed the opportunity to develop closer diplomatic and trade ties to Tibet and China.

velop closer ties with Tibet. In fact, the Russians believed they had a legitimate claim to Tibet based on their conquest of Mongol-held territories centuries earlier. They claimed these territories included Tibet. The Dalai Lama also began to favor an alliance with Russia. His tutor—a Russian-born Mongol named Aguan Porjier—represented Tibet in talks with the Russian czar. When the British heard that Tibet was thinking of forming an alliance with Russia, the British government felt threatened and took immediate action.

To defend British political and economic interests in Tibet, Sir Francis Younghusband led an invasion of the region in 1904. Although the British government had

Millions of Chinese were killed during the Taiping Rebellion, a 14-year battle against the Chinese imperial government. The Chinese above died at the Taku Forts, near Beijing.

Hutton Getty/Liaison Agency

ordered Younghusband and his men to minimize casualties, Tibetans fiercely fought his advance and refused to surrender peaceably. The British, however, quickly defeated the Tibetan soldiers, who were armed with crude weapons and equipment. In their march to Lhasa, Younghusband's men killed at least 300 Tibetans while only 40 British lost their lives.

The Younghusband invasion helped Britain establish closer ties to Tibet. Yet the relationship was tenuous at best. Britain seemed to seesaw between wanting to maintain a genuine political and economic relationship with Tibet and simply using Tibet as part of a larger strategy to fortify its position and interests in Asia. Tibet's future as an independent nation hung in the balance.

SHIFTING ALLIANCES
Immediately following the Younghusband expedition, a series of diplomatic initiatives involving Britain, Tibet, and China set the stage for a major shift in Tibet's relationship with China. Britain signed two treaties to secure its interest in India and in Ti-

bet. The Anglo-Tibetan Convention—ratified at Simla, India, in November 1904 by Tibet and Britain but not by China—established closer ties between Britain and Tibet. The treaty ensured that Britain would be part of any future negotiations regarding Tibet's relationship with China. In return for keeping foreign powers from interfering in Tibetan affairs, Tibet agreed to give up any relations with foreign states other than Britain.

This was good news to Ti-

The Younghusband expedition, led by Sir Francis Younghusband (above, standing in middle), *invaded Tibet in 1904 and helped Britain forge closer ties with Tibet.*

Hulton Getty/Liaison Agency

betans. They believed a closer relationship with Britain would hamper China's ability to threaten Tibet's independence. But Britain continued to recognize Chinese authority over Tibet. In 1906 China and Britain met in Beijing, where they signed an agreement known as the Anglo-Chinese Convention. In effect, the agreement reversed the most important elements of the 1904 convention. Under the Anglo-Chinese Convention, Britain agreed that all negotiations concerning Tibet would from then on be conducted solely with the Chinese, provided that no other foreign powers (mainly Russia) were allowed into Tibet.

CHINA INVADES TIBET
It soon became clear that the Chinese regarded the 1906 treaty and Britain's wavering stance as a green light to take control of Tibet. China fortified military outposts on its eastern border with Tibet and built transportation and phone lines into the region. Tibetans bristled at the move; there was little they could do. By 1909 the Chinese military had secured control over eastern Tibet.

Major Blunder

Why had Britain signed two contradictory agreements? Some British leaders wondered the same thing and regarded the 1906 treaty as a major blunder. Yet there were reasons for the wavering policy. Some British diplomats did not fully grasp the subtle, complex nature of Tibet's relationship with China. The situation was confusing to outsiders. It was clear that China played an important role in Tibet and that Chinese leaders believed Tibet to be under their control. Yet the Tibetans did not regard the Chinese as their masters. They saw China and Tibet as closely linked by history, as close relatives in the same family—not as master and slave. Ultimately, Britain backed away from its relationships with China and Tibet and chose not to pursue closer business or diplomatic ties. The British were more concerned about the impact of their Asian treaties on Russia than they were about any consequences for China or Tibet. In the early 1900s, China appeared to be a weak and ineffective country that posed little danger to British interests.

In early 1910, China's emperor marched 2,000 troops into Tibet to take over the region for good. Tibetan soldiers, led by the Thirteenth Dalai Lama, fought against the Chinese takeover. But, as in the past, Tibet's meager armed forces were no match for the Chinese, who had reached Lhasa by February 1910.

Tibetan leaders strenuously objected to the Chinese invasion. For the first time in Tibet's history, they openly appealed for help from the outside world. The Dalai Lama called for European countries to insist that China withdraw its troops. Although the British verbally protested the invasion, they didn't try to stop China, maintaining that China had **sovereignty** over Tibet. The Dalai Lama barely managed to flee to India before the Chinese reached the Potala Palace.

The Chinese invasion of 1910 marked a crucial turning point in Tibetan-Chinese relations. The Tibetan government refused to accept China's authority. The Dalai Lama and many of his leading ministers established a government-in-exile in India. The Panchen Lama wouldn't obey Chinese demands that he lead a temporary administration. And the Tibetan National Assembly, which maintained contact with the Dalai Lama, sent messages through him denouncing the Chinese, who chose to honor the terms of the assembly's agreements with China and Russia. Britain in effect recognized China's control.

THE CHINESE REVOLUTION

In 1911 a revolution began in China that would topple the Manchu dynasty, which had ruled China for more than 200 years. Under the Qing leadership, the Chinese empire had reached the height of its power. Increasing pressures from European and U.S. powers and widespread political corruption, however, eventually led to the empire's downfall.

The leaders of the Chinese revolution established a new republican government, replacing the emperor and his court with a parliament and a president. The president of the new Republic of China immediately proclaimed that all former imperial lands—including Tibet—still belonged to China.

When Chinese troops arrived at the Chinese-Tibetan border to reestablish Chinese authority, Tibetan troops were there to meet them. The Tibetans fought to maintain their independence and did manage to stop the Chinese advance along the Mekong and Salween Rivers. Meanwhile, imperial Chinese troops still stationed in Lhasa rebelled against their officers. Some of the soldiers went back to China, while others looted Tibetan villages. Tibetan troops fought back and were able to win decisively against the divided

In an atlas published in Shanghai in 1910, the Qing [rulers] for the first time showed Tibet as a part of China.

—Lee Feignon

and leaderless Chinese forces.

By the end of 1912, Tibetan opposition groups expelled the Chinese troops from Tibet. The Chinese government regarded Tibet as one of its provinces. Meanwhile, in 1913, the Thirteenth Dalai Lama formally declared his country's independence and broke all other ties with China. He returned from exile and resumed his leadership of Tibetan spiritual and civic af-

fairs. The Tibetan government reinforced its border areas to block possible Chinese invasions. China also sent troops to the border.

Relations between Tibet and China had reached a standoff. China ignored the declarations of Tibetan independence, which the Tibetans remained equally adamant about maintaining. Tibet's international status remained unclear. To European powers such as Britain, it seemed inevitable that Tibet would eventually fall into China's orbit. China's historic interest in Tibet could not be ignored. And Tibet's

Hulton Getty/Liaison Agency

The Thirteenth Dalai Lama (in carriage) *attended the funeral of Cixi, the dowager empress of China, in 1908. Cixi's death marked the end of the Qing dynasty and the start of a new republic.*

weak military hampered its ability to defend its independence in an increasingly aggressive and competitive world.

A CHANCE FOR PEACE

Britain hoped that Tibet could maintain autonomy over its internal affairs, thereby blunting any threat that Chinese rule could pose to Britain's interests in Asia. In 1913 Britain promoted Tibetan independence by organizing the Simla Convention, a round of negotiations between Tibet and China designed to decide Tibet's future status. At Britain's urging, Tibetan diplomats were willing to make some important concessions—they would accept a certain amount of Chinese control over Tibet, as long as Chinese limits were clearly defined. Privately, they were even willing to acknowledge that Tibet was "an integral part of China," as long as this language did not appear in the main text of a formal treaty. They were concerned that China might later use a signed statement to destroy Tibetan sovereignty.

In exchange for accepting Chinese control over Tibet's foreign and military affairs, Tibetans asked that China allow Tibet to retain control over its domestic affairs, and that China not station troops in Tibet and not make Tibet into a Chinese province. China wanted Tibet and Britain to acknowledge its complete and total sovereignty over Tibet.

In the end, Britain and Tibet developed a closer relationship and signed a new trade agreement during the negotiations. But the central question—the nature of Tibet's relationship to China—remained unanswered. Although Chinese negotiators agreed to the terms of the Simla Convention in principle, China refused to sign the formal agreement.

Power Struggle

During the Chinese revolution of 1911–1912, tradition clashed with new ideas. Although the leaders of the revolution supported the ideals of republican, U.S.-style government, China was not prepared to make the transition to democracy so quickly.

Competing factions struggled for dominance in the postrevolutionary period. A military warlord named Yuan Shikai eventually dissolved the parliament and established a parliamentary democracy. A dictator by temperament and experience, Yuan later sought to reinstate the monarchy and to appoint himself emperor of China. While China remained a republican democracy in name up until Yuan's death in 1916, it was in fact a military dictatorship.

Following World War I (1914–1918) and continuing through the 1920s and 1930s, tension rose between two major factions in China—the Nationalists and the Communists. The Nationalists, led by the movement's founder, Sun Yat-Sen (or Sun Zhongsan), embraced the principles of nationalism, democracy, and socialism. The Communists were inspired by the teachings of Karl Marx and the leadership of Mao Zedong. Their power struggle led to a massive civil war. Mao's Communist Party defeated the Nationalists in 1949.

AN UNCERTAIN INDEPENDENCE

Into the early 1920s, Tibet remained a free and independent state. The Tibetans and the British repeatedly encouraged China to reach a settlement on Tibet. But events thwarted any real diplomatic progress. In 1922 a falling out between the Dalai Lama and the Panchen Lama—the latter refused to pay taxes to support Tibet's military—prompted the Panchen Lama to flee to China. He asked Britain to mediate the dispute. The British turned him down, claiming that they didn't want to interfere in Tibetan affairs. Because of this rift, the Panchen Lama remained in China for 14 years, becoming the center of Chinese plans to divide the Tibetan government. Although he didn't actively participate in the schemes, his decision to leave Tibet stirred suspicions in Lhasa.

A breakdown in Tibet's relationship with Britain also prevented progress on Tibet's status. During the early 1920s, the Dalai Lama had recognized that through a strong relationship with Britain Tibet could counteract China's power. As the relationship improved, the Dalai Lama allowed Britain to begin mining the region's natural resources and to import machinery into Tibet. These new developments caused some Tibetans to worry that the Dalai Lama was being unduly influenced by a foreign power. The Dalai Lama silenced critics by cooling relations with Britain, a move that upset British diplomats who had worked hard to open trade with Tibet.

Meanwhile, Tibet negotiated directly with China. In 1929 and again in 1930, China sent delegations to Lhasa, the second one headed by a Tibetan named Yungon Dzasa. The Dalai Lama and Yungon Dzasa met on friendly terms and discussed the possibility of reaching a direct settlement. In the end, the Dalai Lama was unwilling to compromise on the issue of Tibetan independence and talks failed.

DISRUPTIONS STOP SETTLEMENT

In 1933, after a brief illness, the Thirteenth Dalai Lama died. Renewed attempts to negotiate with China failed. Tibetan negotiators again proposed the terms of the Simla Convention, and China still refused to have anything less than total control over Tibet.

China faced trouble at home once again when Japanese troops invaded in 1936. While at war with Japan, China made several attempts to return the Panchen Lama to Tibet, but he died in December 1937 in China. In 1939, while the search for a new Panchen Lama was underway, Tibetan monks chose a new Dalai Lama, Tenzin Gyatso. But because the Fourteenth Dalai Lama was not yet 18, regents ruled Tibet.

At the dawn of World War II (1939–1945), Tibet and China had not resolved their differences. The war years further delayed any serious efforts to break the stalemate. China's government faced an internal threat, too. The Chinese communist movement, led by Mao Zedong, was gaining popularity.

TIBET'S NEUTRALITY CRISIS

Tibetans generally sympathized with China's difficulties and with the Allied cause during World War II, but the Tibetan government and people remained steadfastly neutral, praying not for the victory of any particular side but for the return of peace.

Despite Tibet's neutral stance, China pressured Tibet to allow the Chinese to construct a military supply route through Tibetan territory. The Tibetan government repeatedly refused to grant China official permission for the construction. But China attempted to build the supply route anyway. Tensions between Tibet and China rose, and Britain offered to mediate.

By this time, Britain had developed a closer relationship with China, and the supply route would benefit the Allied forces (of which both China and Britain were

a part). Britain warned that it would consider withdrawing its support for Tibet if consent for the route was not forthcoming. The Tibetan government still refused to consider any action that would compromise its neutrality. The United States stepped in and prodded Tibet's leaders to drop their opposition. Recognizing that hostilities would increase if they did not concede in some way, Tibet permitted China to transport nonmilitary supplies through Tibet.

Beginning in the mid-1940s, Tibet showed greater interest in ending its traditional isolation. The Tibetan government sent goodwill missions to India, Britain, the United States, and China to

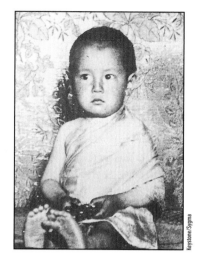

The Thirteenth Dala Lama's death in 1933 prompted a search for his reincarnation. The Fourteenth Dalai Lama (above) *was renamed Tenzin Gyatso.*

congratulate the Allies on their victory and to smooth relations ruffled during the earlier conflict over the military supply route.

When the Tibetans arrived in China, however, Chinese government officials tried to convince the Tibetans to join the Chinese National Assembly, a move that would have signaled acceptance of Chinese authority in Tibet.

The Thirteenth Dalai Lama was the last leader of Tibet to live his whole life in the Potala Palace.

The Tibetans refused to join the assembly.

NEW PLAYERS

In 1947, when Britain granted India its independence, the situation in Tibet changed. Affairs in Asia were suddenly out of Britain's hands, leaving the new government of India to deal with Tibet. Tibet and India agreed to continue relations as set forth by the British, abiding by the terms of the 1914 Simla Convention. At the same time, however, India acknowledged Chinese authority over Tibet without actually denying Tibet's independence. The ambiguity made Tibetans uneasy.

During the same year, the Chinese government went against protocol and chose the new Panchen Lama from a list of ten possible candidates. Because the Dalai Lama traditionally selects the Panchen Lama, Tibet refused to acknowledge the choice.

Meanwhile, dramatic events in China were shaking the world. In the summer of 1949, the Chinese Communist Party (CCP) toppled the weakened Nationalist government and gained control of China, creating the Peo-

1947 Trade Mission

The 1947 Tibetan trade mission stirred controversy by raising the question of Tibet's official status for the countries that the Tibetan delegates visited. Because the Tibetan delegates used Tibetan passports to enter the countries on their itinerary, some have argued that these countries recognized Tibet's independence by meeting with the delegates. Yet this argument is probably overstated. Most countries that accepted the delegates considered the Tibetans to be on unofficial business, not representatives of the Tibetan government. The host countries reported details of the Tibetans' visits to Chinese officials and sometimes insisted Chinese officials be present for meetings.

Mao Zedong illustrates a point while speaking before communist comrades in 1942.

ple's Republic of China (PRC). The communist takeover had a major impact on Tibetan-Chinese relations. During the first half of the twentieth century, China had repeatedly sought to bring Tibet into its fold, and Tibet had successfully resisted. While the two sides had serious disagreements over Tibet's status, both Tibet and China seemed to believe that negotiations and diplomacy were the keys to resolving the issue. The CCP, however, quickly renounced all negotiations over Tibet's future. Then, claiming that all lands formerly under Chinese authority were part of China, the PRC sent troops from the People's Liberation Army (PLA) into Tibet. ⊕

CHAPTER

3

THE PRESENT CONFLICT

In October 1950, China launched a full-scale military assault on Tibet. On Tibet's eastern border, more than 40,000 PLA troops overcame feeble Tibetan resistance and drove toward Lhasa. Over the objections of the Tibetan government and the Dalai Lama—who protested China's actions to the United Nations—China declared that Tibet was officially a part of the PRC.

Many countries around the world denounced the Chinese takeover as a violation of international law and an unjustified act of aggression. But the international community did little else to protest Chinese actions. The United Nations, for example, took no formal action because Tibet was not a member of the United Nations. The U.S. government offered moral support and a safe haven to the Dalai Lama and his government but no military aid.

India, on the other hand, officially recognized the PRC, throwing its support to the Chinese. Facing almost no military opposition, China easily overwhelmed Tibet,

© China Stock

The People's Liberation Army (PLA) entered Tibet on horseback (left, outside of Lhasa), by horse-drawn wagons, and by boat.

killing thousands of ill-equipped Tibetan soldiers.

China declared that, historically, Tibet had always been part of China. China also proclaimed that the current Panchen Lama supported the Chinese invasion. According to China, the Panchen Lama had asked Mao Zedong to "unify the motherland." Again the Tibetan government objected, arguing that Tibet was a sovereign and independent state.

By 1951, however, the PLA had broken what remained of Tibet's military resistance. Despite numerous appeals to the United Nations for support in their struggle for independence, the Tibetan government surrendered to Chinese control. In May 1951, under the threat of further attacks, Tibetan negotiators signed the first treaty between Tibet and China since the Treaty of Uncle and Nephew in A.D. 821. The 1951 17-Point Agreement granted China control over Tibet, with the understanding that the Chinese would leave Tibet's political system intact and would respect the authority of the Dalai Lama.

Tibetan dancers entertained PLA troops near the Potala Palace in 1952.

LIFE UNDER CHINESE RULE

At the beginning of the occupation, the Chinese ruled with restraint, spreading anti-Buddhist propaganda in a relatively quiet manner. By the end of 1954, however, the Chinese had changed their policy. They allowed the Tibetan government to exist but only as puppets for Chinese authority.

Other events further weakened Tibet's position. In April 1954, India signed the Sino-Indian Agreement, under which India gave all the military outposts, telegraph facilities, and rest houses it had built in Tibet to the PRC. The treaty also made frequent references to the "Tibet region" of China. Never before had India openly stated that Tibet was anything but independent. By signing the Sino-Indian Agreement, India publicly acknowledged that Tibet was part of China.

After invading Tibet, China immediately looked for ways to reduce and neutralize the power of the Dalai Lama and the importance of Tibetan Buddhism in Tibet's culture. Chinese authorities elevated the status of the Panchen Lama and took away the political status and privileges of the monks to foment a power struggle and to divide Tibetans into rival factions.

The Chinese presence did benefit the Tibetan people in some ways. For example, China more firmly established western medicine, which the British had introduced in the early 1900s, by opening more hospitals and by providing medical training. The Chinese also improved agricultural productivity with advancements in watering techniques and the breeding of animals.

From 1954 to 1956, relations between Tibet and China were relatively peaceful. There were no violent outbursts or confrontations on either side, although tensions still ran high. In 1954 China invited the Dalai Lama and the Panchen Lama to visit Beijing and to tour other regions of China. During a year-long visit, the Tibetan religious leaders met with Chairman Mao and had optimistic discussions about how Tibet and China could cooperate in the future. The Dalai Lama returned from his visit impressed by China's accomplishments and enthused about his meetings in which Mao had expressed a strong affection for Tibet and a de-

sire to help modernize the country. The Dalai Lama hoped for a peaceful coexistence with the Chinese.

Soon after returning to Lhasa, however, the Dalai Lama found Mao's affection to be false. Chinese military leaders were diverting Tibet's already inadequate food supply to feed their soldiers, while thousands of Tibetans were left to starve.

BITTER RELATIONS

From 1956 onward, the Chinese consolidated their power in Tibet and relations between the Tibetans and

the Chinese steadily deteriorated. China's new policies included confiscating guns from the Tibetan population; imposing new taxes on land, cattle, houses, and other property; and waging a war on Tibetan Buddhism. The Chinese government seized large Tibetan estates, divided them into small plots, and redistributed them. Officials sought to weaken religious influence, which they felt hampered modernization, by terrorizing monks and destroying sacred monasteries.

In response Tibetans formed armed resistance

Mao Zedong (right) *spoke with the Tenth Panchen Lama* (left) *at the end of negotiations in 1951. The resulting agreement gave China power in Tibet, though the Dalai Lama and the Panchen Lama negotiated with Mao throughout the 1950s for more Tibetan autonomy.*

groups in the countryside. By 1956 guerrilla forces were destroying roads and bridges and raiding Chinese supply centers. The Chinese fought back by shelling monasteries that they believed were the centers of the Tibetan resistance. In 1957 Tibetan leaders from Amdo and Kham provinces formed a resistance group called Chushi Gangdruk, which means "Four Rivers Six Ranges" in Tibetan. The group raided Chinese military convoys and gained control of the area south of Lhasa. A growing spirit of resistance led to a major Tibetan-Chinese confrontation.

In the fall of 1958, Tibetans staged a massive rebellion against the Chinese occupation. Tibetan guerrillas defeated 3,000 Chinese troops and seized a key military outpost. During this period, the Chinese repeatedly invited the Dalai Lama to Beijing to meet with top government officials. But the Dalai Lama and his advisers suspected that the Chinese might take him hostage or force him to sign a compromising agreement.

In March 1959, Chinese artillery shells landed near the summer residence of the Dalai Lama. Once again, Chinese officials invited him to a meeting, but this time the offer came from the Chinese military commander in Lhasa, who explicitly told the Dalai Lama to come alone. To the Dalai Lama and his advisers, it seemed like an obvious trap. The Tibetan leader considered fleeing his country to seek refuge in India.

News of the suspicious Chinese invitation aroused a storm of protest among the Tibetan people. Tibetans from all backgrounds—from peasants to monks—poured onto the grounds of the Dalai Lama's summer palace to defend their leader. The crowd built defenses. Within a few days, more than 30,000 Tibetans had gathered to support the Dalai Lama. They called on India to intervene, but the Indian government denied that there was any large-scale violence in Tibet, just a clash of cultures. It saw no need to step in.

When the Chinese fired near the crowd, however, perhaps as a warning to disperse, the Dalai Lama realized his efforts to negotiate had failed. The Dalai Lama and his advisers fled the summer palace and, riding on yaks across the Himalayas, escaped into India.

Many of the Dalai Lama's supporters followed suit, with 100,000 or more Tibetan refugees streaming into India. The Indian government accommodated the refugees in camps, doing their best to settle monks in quiet areas where they could continue to study. The Dalai Lama worked with the Indian government to arrange schooling for children, many

Children were taught that Tibetan religion was blind faith, Tibetan customs and habits 'old green thinking,' Tibetan was a 'useless, backward language,' old Tibetan society was extremely backward, savage, oppressive.

—Tempa Tsering, an official of the Tibetan government-in-exile of whom had been separated from their parents or had been orphaned by the conflict. Instructors taught the children about Tibetan culture and instructed them in Hindi and in English. In most cases, refugees were able to support themselves to some degree. The Indian government saw to it that they received enough food and decent shelter. By the end of 1959, 17,000 Tibetan refugees had settled in India.

THE CHINESE CLAMP DOWN

Following the 1959 uprising, the Chinese dealt harshly with the Tibetan people. Chinese troops launched new attacks on the Tibetan resistance movement. The Chinese replaced the Tibetan government with a military dictatorship led by the Panchen Lama. The new government banned freedom of speech, movement, and association. The Chinese abruptly shut down all communication between Tibet and India.

In the ensuing months and years, China embarked on a broad strategy to prevent future Tibetan resistance. The Chinese sent many of Lhasa's inhabitants to labor camps, where the prisoners worked long hours at manual labor. Each day labor camp prisoners received a small ration of bread and water and were forced to recite communist propaganda. In the camps, many mothers and fathers were separated from their children and never seen or heard from again.

Life was perhaps hardest for Tibet's religious elite. Chinese troops arrested many monks and nuns, who were often beaten, tortured, and even murdered while in custody. Others chose to commit suicide.

Meanwhile, many in the international community voiced strong objections to China's policies in Tibet. The people and press of India protested the most, staging massive demonstrations against the Chinese invasion.

Religion

Since 1950 the Chinese government has regulated the Tibetan religion. Monks and nuns, for example, are subject to some of the worst human rights abuses in Tibet, mostly because they are the best-educated and most-respected segment of Tibetan society and represent the greatest threat to Chinese authority. The Chinese fear their power to rally the Tibetan people against China's rule.

Tibetan Buddhist monks and nuns are the Tibetan elite. These monks are preparing for a ceremony at the Jokhang Temple.

© Dennis Cox/ChinaStock

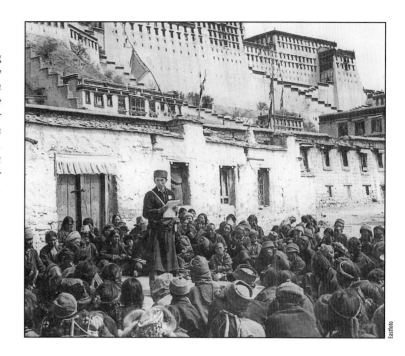

A Tibetan staff member (standing above the crowd) *of the Military Control Committee in Lhasa explained the Chinese government's State Council Order of March 28th (1959) to Tibetan citizens. That same month, Tibetans formed protests against the government's increasing power in Tibet.*

Even newspapers known to support the Indian government, led by Jawaharlal Nehru, criticized it, claiming that by remaining silent about the invasion, Nehru failed to accurately represent the people.

This accusation prompted Nehru to express mild sympathy toward Tibet. China responded vehemently, linking India to Britain's invasion of Tibet in 1904. India expressed concern about Tibetan autonomy. When India welcomed the Dalai Lama as an honored guest, an outraged China again accused India of walking in Britain's footsteps. Nehru likened Chinese rhetoric to a war of words. In the meantime, China also laid claim to 30,000 square miles of Indian territory.

A REIGN OF TERROR

During the early 1960s, the Chinese continued to undermine the historic structure of Tibetan life. Chinese propagandists argued that China was liberating Tibetans from an unfair economic system, under which a minority of monks and nonreligious nobility oppressed the majority of the Tibetan people.

In 1963 the PRC established the Tibet Autonomous Region and even more visibly altered Tibet's traditional economy. They had already divided the large monastic estates into smaller plots. The Chinese then forced farmers to turn over their agricultural products to the government. Instead of the traditional Tibetan barley, the grain that grew best in the region, Chinese authorities ordered farmers to plant wheat, which was favored by the growing number of Chinese troops in Tibet.

Fearing communist oppression and loss of power in Tibet, the Dalai Lama (right, in glasses and hat) fled Lhasa for India in 1959.

Although the Chinese insisted that they were improving opportunities for average Tibetans, for most life became much harder. Upheaval of traditional agricultural techniques led to confusion and famine. Many laborers fled Tibet because of the government's broken promises and meager rations. Thousands of Tibetans died of starvation. In 1963 the Chinese closed Tibet to foreign visitors.

Meanwhile, in 1964, the Panchen Lama refused to play a part in the Chinese puppet government any longer. So the Chinese denounced him and kept him in custody under harsh living conditions.

THE CULTURAL REVOLUTION

The **Cultural Revolution**—a period of rebellion against religious and cultural tradition—swept through China from 1966 to 1976. Conditions in Tibet worsened, as the Chinese combined single farms into communes that produced all of the food for the population. At the same time, China stepped up efforts to purge Tibet of anyone perceived to be an enemy of the state. The PLA

Groups of Tibetan refugees, like the one above, began following the Dalai Lama to India. The majority eventually settled in Dharamsala. This new home of the Dalai Lama is called "Little Lhasa."

imprisoned and tortured suspected enemies to extract more names or information. Chinese authorities labeled Tibetan the "language of religion" and restricted its use and teaching. The government banned books that taught children about their religious heritage and replaced them with books promoting Mao's **communist** doctrines.

Perhaps the most shocking aspect of the Cultural Revolution in Tibet was destruction of the monasteries. In 1966, young communists known as Red Guards, most of whom were Tibetans,

Indian Prime Minister Jawaharlal Nehru (above left) *welcomed the Dalai Lama* (above right) *in Mussoorie, India, shortly after the Dalai Lama arrived there.*

tried to destroy Tibetan culture and individuality. They systematically looted temples, destroying religious books, vessels, and images.

Political arrests during the Cultural Revolution broke up many families, and countless children became orphans after their parents died in prison. To discover and punish those who disagreed with the revolution's ideals, the Chinese held trials, forcing children to accuse parents and friends to accuse friends. Mao's government also banned traditional dress and religious practices.

Some Tibetans openly

Indians joined the Tibetans in taking a stand against China. Outside the Chinese embassy in New Delhi, India, a crowd demonstrated in 1959 against the Chinese government's takeover of Tibet.

defied the Red Guards and the Cultural Revolution. In June 1969, Tibetans all over the country ignored the ban on religion to celebrate Saka Dawa, the anniversary of Buddha's birth, enlightenment, and death. In July, people in Lhasa left work to honor World Solidarity Day, which rejected the ideals of the Cultural Revolution. In Lhoka, 3,000 young Tibetans attacked PLA troops and killed 200 solders. An uprising in the southwestern part of the country killed more than 1,000 Chinese soldiers.

SLIGHT IMPROVEMENTS

By 1971 many Chinese authorities understood that Tibetans would continue to revolt unless the Chinese loosened their grip. China allowed Tibetans to wear traditional clothing and relaxed restrictions on travel and religious practices. The Chinese government even began secret talks with the Dalai Lama.

In 1974 the CCP sent a special delegation to Tibet to improve relations. The Chinese blamed Tibet's poor economic condition on Lin Biao, a high-ranking communist who was the defense minister of China from 1959 to 1971. Then they declared amnesty, appointed Tibetans to lead village communes, and patched some of the damage done to famous holy sites. The Chinese also called for refugees to return and gradually opened doors to foreigners.

The first visitors—a select group of tourists including leading international journalists and western scholars—provided detailed accounts of life in Tibet under Chinese rule. Lhasa, they said, had become two cities—a poor, underdeveloped old section where 50,000 Tibetans lived, and a new town where more than 70,000 Chinese newcomers made their homes. Some tourists

The Chinese government published propaganda pictures like this one of rural Tibetan peasant farmers in 1965. The CCP claims that communist reforms have improved peasants' lives by introducing communal farming methods and livestock raising.

Corbis/Bettmann-UPI

Cultural Revolution

In 1966 Mao Zedong hoped to abolish slow bureaucracy and to promote an efficient form of communism. To accomplish this goal, he started the Cultural Revolution, a movement that aimed to completely recreate China's culture.

During the revolution, which lasted from 1966 to 1976, Mao inspired Chinese students known as Red Guards to attack all aspects of traditional society. Under his orders, most of China's universities closed, and students were encouraged to learn from peasants living in communes. Red Guards publicly humiliated teachers and intellectuals, sending them to communes or to hard-labor camps as punishment for teaching students about traditional culture. The movement eventually spread to Tibet, where Tibetans themselves joined the Red Guards' ranks.

As many as 100 million people throughout China died as a direct result of the Cultural Revolution. In the end, Mao's revolution damaged the Chinese government and economy so badly that he was forced to call in the PLA to restore order.

The Cultural Revolution was a countrywide overhaul of lifestyle for the Chinese. Under Mao's fervent guidance, Red Guards dressed in the blue of "common people" and marched through city streets, calling out Mao's ideas for reform. Red Guards hoped to do away with the intellectual elite by holding public "criticisms." Here they are hanging a humiliating sign on an educated man and parading him around the town of Harbin.

© Li Zhensheng/ChinaStock

CIA Involvement

From 1959 to 1971, the U.S. Central Intelligence Agency (CIA) did its part to stop the spread of communism by training Tibetan resistance groups. The CIA secretly flew Tibetans to training camps in the Rocky Mountains of Colorado. In fact, many recruits didn't even know they were in the United States. After a series of tough training sessions, U.S. pilots dropped the recruits, complete with weapons, radios, and suicide pills, into Tibet. From bases along Tibet's borders with Nepal and India, resistance troops worked to distract the PLA. In 1971—after President Richard Nixon renewed U.S. relations with the PRC—the U.S. government stopped the resistance training.

Under communist rule, more schools opened in Tibet and some Tibetans who had been peasants could pursue an education, like these students at Lhasa Secondary School.

noted that the Chinese treated Tibetans with open contempt. Food, clothing, and other goods were strictly rationed. Chinese shopkeepers seemed to operate most stores. Children still worked long hours in the fields instead of going to school. Roads were in poor condition.

THE STANDOFF CONTINUES

By the time Mao Zedong died in 1976, the Cultural Revolution had ended and China had moderated its stance on Tibet. Mao's successor, Deng Xiaoping, eased some of the government's most restrictive policies in Tibet and in other parts of China in 1979. The Chinese government allowed teachers to teach the Tibetan language in schools again, albeit on an extremely limited basis. That same year, Deng expressed an interest in starting talks with the Dalai Lama. The Chinese leader indicated that "except for the independence of Tibet, all other questions can be negotiated."

While this declaration fell short of Tibetans' desire for a free and independent Tibet, the Dalai Lama saw it as a positive step. Many Tibetans, including the Dalai Lama, hoped this was a sign that

The Chinese Communist Party selected Mao's comrade Deng Xiaoping (left) to succeed Mao in 1976. That year marked the end of the Cultural Revolution and the beginning of slow but massive democratic and economic reforms. Deng is credited with the "opening" of China to new policies concerning trade, business practices, public policy, and cultural influences.

China would begin to treat Tibetans more humanely. The Chinese government allowed the Dalai Lama to send several fact-finding missions to Tibet so he might judge for himself how the Chinese were treating his people.

During this thaw in Tibetan-Chinese relations, the Dalai Lama privately developed a peace proposal he called "the middle way"—a compromise that, in many respects, was similar to the terms proposed by Tibetan diplomats at the Simla Conference in 1913. Tibet would agree to remain part of China and to grant the Chinese authority over foreign policy if the Chinese would allow Tibetans to control their own domestic affairs. Once again, however, the talks fell apart. The Chinese failed to respond to the Dalai Lama's proposals and insisted that the only way to resolve the conflict was for him to return to Tibet and to accept a nominal post in the Chinese government. This was unacceptable to the Dalai Lama.

By the early 1980s, the Chinese realized that many of their policies—such as the implementation of the commune system—had failed in Tibet. The Chinese granted Tibetans more freedom. They abolished taxes in rural areas and closed down the communes. They allowed Tibetan farmers to grow barley again instead of wheat, recognizing that barley is more suitable to Tibet's climate. In 1981 the Chinese reopened 45 Tibetan monasteries. Parents again began sending their children to monastic schools, and religious institutions regained importance in people's lives. The government allowed families to return to subsistence farming, and agricultural production rose substantially.

The government also initiated 43 major projects in Tibet, most to benefit the tourism industry. It passed the Law on **Regional Autonomy** for Minority Nationalities, which allowed Chinese immigrants to move to Tibet to work on the new projects.

In 1985 the Chinese appointed Wu Jinghua as head of the Tibetan Communist Party. Wu was a member of the Yi ethnic group, which is closely related to the Tibetans. He appeared in Tibetan dress at religious ceremonies and made donations to monks. Under Wu's leadership, Lhasa's streets were renamed using their old Tibetan names. Wu, who did not speak Tibetan himself, encouraged all officers under his command to learn Tibetan.

But improved living conditions did little to soften the relationship between Tibetans and Chinese. Some Chinese police and military officers were quick to respond harshly to the slightest

Five-Point Peace Plan

Over the past two decades, the Dalai Lama and other Tibetan government-in-exile officials have proposed many solutions to the Tibetan-Chinese conflict. In September 1987, the Dalai Lama introduced the following Five-Point Peace Plan at a meeting of the Congressional Human Rights Caucus in Washington, D.C. The terms of this proposal essentially matched his earlier proposal outlined in Strasbourg, France. China's leaders have refused to consider the terms of this compromise or of any proposal that falls short of complete, unconditional acceptance of Chinese sovereignty over Tibet.

FIVE-POINT PEACE PLAN

1. Transformation of the whole of Tibet into a zone of peace;

2. Abandonment of China's population transfer policy which threatens the very existence of the Tibetans as a people;

3. Respect for the Tibetan people's fundamental human rights and democratic freedoms;

4. Restoration and protection of Tibet's natural environment and the abandonment of China's use of Tibet for the production of nuclear weapons and dumping of nuclear waste;

5. Commencement of earnest negotiations on the future status of Tibet and of relations between the Tibetan and Chinese peoples.

provocation. Tibetans often lashed out against police brutality with more violence.

In September 1987, after the Dalai Lama spoke to the U.S. Human Rights Subcommittee about human rights abuses in Tibet, monks at the Sera Monastery protested in the streets of

Lhasa. The PRC had denounced the speech, and its police responded by beating demonstrators, acts that further upset the citizens of Lhasa. In October the Chinese police arrested another group of protesters. When protesters raided the Lhasa police station to demand that the monks be released, the police fought back, killing several marchers. Both sides backed off, and, although tensions still ran high, the violence subsided.

A CHANCE AT PEACE

Less than a year later, in June 1988, the Dalai Lama spoke to the European Parliament in Strasbourg, France. In the speech, the Dalai Lama announced that he would accept less than full independence for Tibet. In the hope of bringing peace to Tibet, the Dalai Lama proposed that China be allowed to retain control over Tibet's foreign relations and to station troops in the region. In exchange, Tibet would elect a democratic government to handle domestic affairs. By stating to such a large audience that he would accept nominal Chinese sovereignty over Tibet, the Dalai Lama

had made a big concession to Beijing. But China rejected the proposal. It objected to the Dalai Lama's reference to a once-independent Tibet and to the Dalai Lama's insistance that a foreign lawyer be present for negotiations. Tibetan radicals weren't happy with the proposal either. They thought that the Dalai Lama was giving too much to the Chinese.

Violence erupted again on December 10, 1988, when

about 30 Tibetans marched into the center of Lhasa. They were angry that Chinese authorities had canceled a visit by the Dalai Lama. There are conflicting reports of what happened next. The Chinese claim that police fired shots into the air to scare away the protesters. But reports from foreign travelers state that the police fired directly into the crowd, killing one and injuring 13 people.

Inflamed feelings of resentment toward Chinese rule in Tibet and worldwide discussions on China's human rights abuses led to protests in Lhasa in 1987.

In March 1989, on the thirtieth anniversary of the Lhasa uprising, pro-independence rallies erupted in Tibet. Chinese troops cracked down hard, killing 16 protesters and placing Tibet under strict **martial law.**

During the next year, the Chinese executed as many as 2,000 Tibetans. Later in the same year, the Panchen Lama announced that Tibetans had paid too high of a price for modernization. Shortly after making this statement, the Panchen Lama died of a heart attack.

We should wage a tit-for-tat struggle against the Dalai clique's sabotage. We should, once again, stage another campaign across Tibet to thoroughly expose and criticize the Dalai clique, heighten our alertness and strengthen preventive measures so as to keep the situation stable.

—Tibet's government-controlled radio proclamation after the December 1996 bombing

Many Tibetans suspected foul play.

In October 1989, the Dalai Lama won the Nobel Peace Prize for his efforts to end the conflict with China. China responded by denouncing the Nobel Prize Committee for meddling in China's internal affairs. Meanwhile, growing unrest over economic problems in China spilled over into Tibet and combined with Tibetans' discontent over Chinese rule to spark a new round of protests, riots, and demonstrations. This cycle of protests and violent crackdowns continued into the next decade.

In the early 1990s, the Chinese replaced progressive Tibetan Communist Party leader Wu Jinghua with reformer Hu Jintao. In 1992 the Chinese government brought Hu into the CCP. Chen Guiyuan replaced Hu in Tibet and started a new economic program.

AP/Wide World Photos

The Dalai Lama won the Nobel Peace Prize in 1989 for his efforts to keep peace with China while working toward independence for Tibet.

As part of the plan, the Chinese opened Tibet to outside investment in 1992. By 1993 the Chinese government had approved contracts with 41 foreign companies who hoped to invest in Tibet. Although the standard of living for most Tibetans improved with the latest round of economic development, most of the new businesses were in the hands of Han Chinese. Tibetans continue to lag behind their Han counterparts in education, employment opportunities, and pay.

By 1995 negotiations seemed to take a giant step backward when the Dalai Lama declared that, after a six-year search, Tibetan monks had discovered the new Panchen Lama in Tibet, a young boy named Gedhun Choekyi Nyima. The Chinese refused to acknowledge the choice and denounced the Dalai Lama. They took the boy into custody in Beijing and selected a new Panchen Lama, Gyaltsen Norbu, themselves.

In the meantime, violence continued to rock Tibet. In December 1996, for example, a bomb blast shattered the pre-dawn quiet in a popular Lhasa shopping district. The force of the explosion, outside a city government office building, wounded two night watchmen and several shopkeepers who lived nearby. Although no group claimed responsibility for the attack, Chinese authorities immediately blamed it on the Tibetan resistance movement and the Dalai Lama.

In January and March of 1996, other bombs damaged the house of a lama said to be a Chinese sympathizer and the main gate of the Communist Party headquarters. The explosions may be signs that the Tibetan resistance movement has grown impatient with the lack of improvement in human rights conditions in Tibet and with the Chinese government's unwillingness to engage in serious dialogue with the Dalai Lama.

To the Chinese, the bombings were the acts of Tibetan terrorists, and a justification for even harsher restrictions on Tibetan culture, religion, and personal freedoms. Others believe that the Chinese may have planted the bombs themselves to make their repressive policies appear

Tibetans prayed for the release of the Dalai Lama's choice for the Eleventh Panchen Lama after Chinese authorities took him into custody.

In the late 1980s, activists ransacked a Chinese restaurant (above) *during pro-independence rioting in Lhasa.*

justified and to sow discord among the ranks of Tibetan resistance groups.

In the late 1990s, the Chinese maintained their tight hold on Tibet. Although tourism has increased, undercover Chinese police continue to monitor Lhasa's streets in the event of a riot. Tibetans and foreign visitors must watch what they say and do while in public. Un-dercover police also pose as monks in monasteries.

Observers speculated that the change in leadership when Deng Xiaoping died in 1997 would usher in a new Tibetan policy. Many of China's communist leaders who've instigated and enforced Tibetan policy are growing old and dying. Deng's successor, Jiang Zemin, has since forged ahead with economic reforms, going so far as to close state-owned factories and to push them into private hands. But for the most part, Jiang has stuck with Deng's policies.

As human rights groups continue to monitor the situation in Tibet into the next century, the world waits and hopes for an end to the conflict. ⊕

Fulbright Scholar Seized

The threat of arrest and detention is a fact of life for millions of Tibetans living under Chinese rule. During the 1990s, the government's aggressive efforts to stifle dissent have increasingly drawn international attention.

In July 1995, Ngawang Choephel, a Tibetan music teacher and scholar studying as a Fulbright scholar at Middlebury College in Vermont, left on a trip to Tibet. A musicologist who specializes in studying and recording traditional Tibetan folk music, Ngawang Choephel went to Tibet to conduct research for a documentary film he was helping to prepare.

In August 1995, about one month after arriving in Tibet, however, he was reported missing. More than a year later, the Chinese admitted that they were holding him in detention. The Chinese had charged him with spying for the Dalai Lama and with breaking China's state security laws. Although the Chinese presented no evidence for his crime, he was not allowed any visitors. This is a clear violation of United Nations protocol on the treatment of prisoners.

In December 1996, the Chinese government tried Ngawang Choephel and convicted him of being a spy. The court sentenced him to 18 years in prison. To draw attention to the injustice of this case—and to the thousands of political prisoners being held in Tibet—Amnesty International produced a film titled *Missing in Tibet*. Prominent musicians such as Paul McCartney, David Bowie, and Sting signed a petition calling on the Chinese to release the music scholar.

© Robert Fried

Shops with stereos and silk for sale are a common sight in Lhasa.

CHAPTER

4

WHAT'S BEING DONE TO SOLVE THE PROBLEM

With the amount of media attention given to Tibet in recent years—most of which focuses on human rights issues and refugee aid—it's easy to lose sight of the actual problem that keeps the conflict going. For hundreds of years, Tibet and China have clashed over who should control and live in Tibet. To resolve the conflict, both sides need to come to

the negotiating table, willing to compromise. So far that hasn't happened.

POINTS OF CONTENTION

As recently as December 1997, the Dalai Lama cited the ongoing dispute over Tibet's historic relationship with China as a major obsta-

cle to holding further negotiations about Tibet's future. In October 1997, during his visit to the United States, Chinese president Jiang Zemin repeated his conditions for engaging in negotiations. The Dalai Lama must firmly reject the Tibetan independence movement and

Tibetan immigrants in the United States protested Chinese president Jiang Zemin's visit to Washington, D.C., in 1997. They demanded the release of the Panchen Lama and greater sanctions against China for its human rights abuses.

must acknowledge that, even historically, Tibet has always been a part of China.

While for many years the Dalai Lama has stated a willingness to accept Chinese sovereignty over Tibet, he refuses to accept these terms. "I am ready to unite with China," the Dalai Lama said in a recent statement. "What is past, is past, I don't want to bring it up again. But how can I ever say that Tibet has never been independent? That would be a lie."

Since the Chinese invaded Tibet, the Dalai Lama has asked for no less than total independence for Tibet. By conceding sovereignty to China and asking in return for a degree of autonomy in domestic affairs, he has made a big compromise. Some outside observers have expressed hopes that China will accept the offer and will end the conflict once and for all. But China's response has not been forthcoming.

APPLYING PRESSURE

To push China into action, countries such as Germany and the United States have pressured China to improve its treatment of Tibetans and to hold serious discussions

A Focus on Tibet

In July 1997, President Clinton approved the creation of a new position in the State Department called special coordinator on Tibetan affairs. Gregory Craig, the first appointment to the position, was in charge of promoting constructive dialogue between the Chinese government and the Dalai Lama and monitoring human rights conditions in Tibet. Mr. Craig's focus also included preservation of Tibetan heritage. The timing of the Craig appointment was a significant statement of support for Tibet. Craig was officially named to fill the position while the President of China, Jiang Zemin, was in the United States on a rare visit to meet with President Clinton, leading members of Congress, and others.

In January 1999, Julia Taft, Assistant Secretary for Population, Refugees and Migration, took over the post. Response to Taft's appointment varied. The Tibetan government-in-exile welcomed Taft and hoped that she would be able to foster negotiations between the Chinese government and the Dalai Lama. The Chinese government was strongly opposed to the appointment. The PRC reasoned that Tibet is a part of China and the region's problems are part of China's internal affairs in which other countries should refrain from becoming involved.

with the Dalai Lama and his government.

In June 1996, the German Bundestag (parliament) passed a resolution condemning China's human rights abuses in Tibet. Germany later hosted an international conference on Tibet. The Dalai Lama and other Tibetan leaders attended the event, despite Chinese threats to reduce trade if the conference took place in Germany. Although Germany is China's largest European trading partner, the German government did not back down, and the conference proceeded as planned.

In September 1996, seven members of the German parliament's Foreign Relations Subcommittee on Human Rights toured Tibet to assess the human rights situation. Members of the group hoped that their visit would

Jiang Zemin

Jiang Zemin is the president of the People's Republic of China, the general secretary of the Chinese Communist Party, and the chairman of the Communist Party's Central Military Commission. Born in 1926 in the town of Yangzhou in Jiangsu province, Jiang studied electrical engineering and managed several factories before becoming the vice minister of various state commissions and the minister of electronics industry (1980–1985). He was appointed to the politburo in 1987 after serving a stint as Shanghai's mayor. In 1989 Deng Xiaoping appointed Jiang general secretary of the CCP, which came as a surprise to many officials. He has been president since 1993.

Jiang has consistently followed Deng's reform policies for China, hoping for further economic development of the country. He is knowledgeable and respectful of Western culture, literature, and music and has been seen singing exuberantly and dancing in public. Jiang has been labeled practical, an opportunist, and even "the Weathervane" for making decisions that are acceptable to all—including strict communists and those who support the continual opening of China. On the issue of Tibet, however, Jiang has stated, "No country has this special privilege to interfere in the internal affairs of other countries or impose its will upon others."

Chinese president Jiang Zemin (left) *meets U.S. president Bill Clinton* (right) *at a press conference in 1997.*

Jiang showed his dual nature again when he traveled through Tibet in 1998. He reportedly said to his companions, "Let's try to do something that will really help the Tibetans out, rather then just offering cheap words of support." Once in Lhasa, however, he is said to have told TAR political leaders to "take resolute and effective measures to rebuff the disturbances caused by separatists." Jiang's stance is clearly on the side of the CCP: Tibet has always been part of China and should remain so.

lead to further dialogue on Tibet between Germany and China and, in time, better conditions in Tibet.

During the 1980s and 1990s, U.S. opposition to China's policies in Tibet has increased with growing public awareness. In October 1987, for example, the U.S. Senate responded to violent protests in Tibet by voting 98-0 to make future arms sales to China dependent on improvements in human

Dalai Lama

The Fourteenth Dalai Lama was born Lhamo Dhondrub in the town of Taktser in Qinghai province, China. In 1937, at the age of two, he was identified by a search party of Tibetan monks as the reincarnation of Chenrezi, the Dalai Lama. He was renamed Tenzin Gyatso in 1940. The Dalai Lama lived in the Potala Palace in Lhasa as the political and spiritual leader of Tibet until 1959. Since then he has lived in Dharamsala, India (called "Little Lhasa"), where many Tibetan Buddhists who have followed him also reside. The Dalai Lama is an active teacher of Tibetan Buddhism. He has also become a leader to many non-Buddhists throughout the world who admire his philosophies and ethics. He lectures on topics related to peace worldwide and won the Nobel Peace Prize in 1989.

His Holiness the Dalai Lama preaches in Dharamsala, India, and gives lectures worldwide on topics related to peace.

In 1988 the Dalai Lama finally proposed to the Chinese government that China grant Tibet internal autonomy—as the name "Tibet Autonomous Region" suggests—and even keep PLA troops in the province. Though his proposal was the first to show a more moderate stance on the issue, it was rejected. He retains, "I have been making every effort over the years to facilitate negotiations with the Chinese government."

The Dalai Lama still hopes fervently to return to his home in the Potala Palace once Tibet is declared an independent country. In addition, he and his followers call for a democratic government, though such a government would effectively no longer look to him as Tibet's leader. The Dalai Lama has said, "I hold the firm belief that it is possible for us to find a mutually acceptable and beneficial solution on the Tibetan question."

rights conditions in Tibet.

In 1990 Congress added an amendment to an immigration bill that allowed 1,000 Tibetan refugees to resettle in the United States. Although the United States officially considers Tibet part of China, the U.S. Congress passed a resolution in 1991 stating that Tibet was an independent nation prior to the Chinese invasion in 1950. The resolution also recognized the Tibetan government-in-exile as the legitimate representative of Tibet.

More recently, the U.S. House and Senate have passed numerous resolutions on Tibet. Although these resolutions are only symbolic, they convey a renewed interest in Tibet and a focus on the difficulties its people face. In 1997 Joint Resolution 43 of the 104th Congress, for example, stated that the United States should pressure China to release political prisoners, to honor the Dalai Lama's selection of the new Panchen Lama, Gedhun Choekyi Nyima, and to ensure his safety.

IMPOSING SANCTIONS

Some U.S. politicians believe that the best way to get China to change its attitude on Tibet is to impose economic sanctions. Experts on China agree that tough action is the only way to make Chinese leaders understand. They argue that China will continue its policies in Tibet as long as it faces no economic penalties for doing so. In a recent public opinion poll, more than two-thirds of Americans surveyed supported this view. Yet this is a controversial issue.

The Clinton administration has since backed away from a policy of linking human rights improvements in China and Tibet to trade. The government argues that the best way to bring about change in China is by continuing to trade with China and to treat the country with respect. Many of these efforts, however, have fallen flat. Time after time, China has ignored formal requests to halt human rights abuses, only to find that Europe and North America appear unwilling to reprimand China for not meeting their demands.

EFFORTS TO HELP TIBET

Grassroots organizations from all over the world have sought to build international support for the Tibetans and Tibetan refugees. Human rights groups such as the International Campaign for

The Dalai Lama's picture is illegal in Tibet, but, in defiance of this law, his image is for sale at booths at the Barkhor market in Lhasa.

© Kurt Thorson

Facing page: *Tibet's boundaries have been in dispute for centuries. Tibet in 1930 (top) was considerably smaller than in 1963, when it was named Xizang province or Tibet Autonomous Region (middle). The Dalai Lama and Tibetans hope the Chinese government will relinquish its claim on Tibet as a province and allow it to become an independent country.*

Tibet in 1930

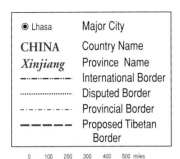

◉ Lhasa — Major City
CHINA — Country Name
Xinjiang — Province Name
— · — · — International Border
· · · · · · · · · · Disputed Border
— · · — · · — Provincial Border
— — — — Proposed Tibetan Border

0   100   200   300   400   500 miles
0   100 200 300 400 500 kilometers

Tibet in 1963

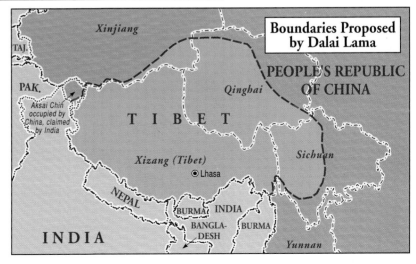

Boundaries Proposed by Dalai Lama

Help from the Stars

A long list of movie stars including Richard Gere, Steven Seagal, and Harrison Ford, along with musical groups such as R.E.M., Pearl Jam, Patti Smith, and The Beastie Boys, have used their influence and popularity to draw attention to Tibetans' ongoing struggle. These and other American celebrities have also helped raise money to help Tibetan refugees by promoting fundraisers, live concerts, and albums such as "Long Live Tibet" (released in 1997).

For the past four years, Adam Yauch—a member of the Beastie Boys and co-founder of the pro-Tibetan independence organization The Milarepa Fund—has organized the Tibetan Freedom Concert. On June 13, 1999, the fourth annual Tibetan Freedom Concert was held in four cities around the world—Amsterdam, Tokyo, Sydney, and Milwaukee. The concerts have raised more than two million dollars. Profits are used to conduct political and educational campaigns about Tibet.

Reuters/Larry Downing/Archive Photos

Actor Richard Gere (in gray suit) *joined Tibetan monks at a "Free Tibet" rally in 1998. Gere is an activist for Tibetan independence and is the chairperson of the International Campaign for Tibet.*

Tibet (ICT), the Tibetan Centre for Human Rights and Democracy (TCHRD), and many others have raised public awareness of China's human rights abuses in Tibet. At the same time, these organizations have raised substantial funds to supply Tibetan refugees with food, water, and shelter.

The ICT, a nonprofit organization based in Washington, D.C., gathers information on Tibet from fact-finding trips and interviews with Chinese and Tibetan exiles. It promotes news coverage of Tibet, testifies before Congress and the United Nations on issues concerning Tibet, and publishes two newsletters—the *Tibet Press Watch* and *Ti-*

betan Environment & Development News.

The TCHRD, based in Dharamsala, India, recently drew UN attention to reports that China is coercing Tibetan women to practice birth control against their will—a policy that violates Article 16 of the United Nations Convention on the Elimination of All Forms of

Discrimination Against Women. The group has also been a strong advocate for the rights and well-being of political prisoners in Tibet and has sponsored numerous letter-writing campaigns on their behalf.

EFFORTS IN CHINA

Over the past decade, China's experiences with the Dalai Lama and his government-in-exile have made it difficult for the PRC to trust the Tibetan leaders. Both sides have allowed pride to interfere with efforts to solve the conflict. The Chinese government believes that the Dalai Lama often makes decisions based upon what will make China look bad in the European and American media. So in the late 1990s, the Chinese government has not attempted to negotiate with the Dalai Lama, believing that the Tibetan leader isn't willing to make the kind of compromise that would be acceptable to the PRC. Many PRC hard-liners favor waiting for the Dalai Lama—who was 64 in 1999—to die before trying to resolve the conflict with Tibet.

With the TAR firmly in its grasp, the PRC has pushed forward with economic development in the region. To secure its business interests, the PRC has maintained a strong police force in Lhasa. By keeping the peace and discouraging riots, China hopes to attract international business to Tibet.

TAKING ACTION

Some organizations, such as the London-based Free Tibet Campaign, Students for a Free Tibet (SFT), Tibet Education Action, and the Tibet Youth Congress, have taken a more aggressive stance. The Free Tibet Campaign, for example, has strongly supported economic and political sanctions against China and has boycotted companies doing business in Tibet. In August 1997, Holiday Inn pulled out of Tibet after the group sponsored a long boycott of the hotel.

Students for a Free Tibet (SFT), an organization of U.S. college students, is a strong advocate of Tibetan independence. Chapters of the group at college campuses around the country sponsor Tibetan speakers and cultural activities, engage in letter-writing campaigns in support of Tibetan human rights, and organize protests and boycotts against companies doing business in Tibet. In early 1999, SFT sponsored a postcard campaign to pressure China to free the Panchen Lama. The group sent postcards to Jiang Zemin and to the UN's High Commissioner for Human Rights.

Three members of the Tibet Youth Congress staged a hunger strike in front of the UN's building in Geneva, Switzerland, in April 1999. The trio demanded that the UN send a commission to investigate the Panchen Lama's situation and to pressure China to release political prisoners in Tibet. After 26 days of fasting, the members of the Tibet Youth Congress broke the strike. By this time, the UN had promised to talk about possible solutions to the Panchen Lama crisis at their May-June 1999 meeting. The committee also said that it would talk to the Chinese government about releasing several high-profile Tibetan political prisoners. At the end of the strike, the Tibet Youth Congress announced that it believed its efforts had forced the UN and the international community to take action in Tibet.

CHAPTER 4   *What's Being Done to Solve the Problem*

REFUGEE STORIES

In addition to tending to the obvious needs of Tibetan refugees—such as providing them with food and shelter—volunteers have given some refugees something much more valuable. In 1995 Pam Maykut, a psychology professor at Viterbo College in Ferryville, Wisconsin, taught English to Tibetan refugee children at the Tibetan Home School in Mussoorie, India. Toward the end of the three-month class, Maykut asked the youngsters to tell the story of their escape from Tibet. She gave them some paint and canvas and asked them to create images of what they couldn't put into words.

Maykut told a reporter for the *Minneapolis Star Tribune* that the pictures were "much more powerful than words." One portrayed the escape of three young Tibetan girls who ran into trouble when border guards from Nepal took all of their money before the girls could escape across the Indian border. In another painting, an eight-year-old boy depicted his journey out of Tibet. During his escape he was

United Nations Efforts in Tibet

To gain support and sympathy for its cause, the Tibetan government-in-exile has sought to forge closer ties with other nations, particularly with the powerful countries of western Europe and with the United States. Leaders of the Tibetan government-in-exile, including the Dalai Lama, have shared their views with the people and leaders of these and many other nations. Tibetan leaders have urged the representatives of democratic countries—and the United Nations—to pressure China to improve human rights conditions in Tibet, to halt the destruction of Tibet's unique culture, and to negotiate a peaceful settlement to the ongoing conflict between Tibet and China.

Recently, UN groups have become more actively involved in Tibet. In the early 1990s, for example, the United Nations Sub-Commission on Prevention of Discrimination and Protection of Minorities passed a resolution calling on the Chinese government "fully to respect the fundamental human rights and freedoms of the Tibetan people." With this declaration, the commission became the first UN body since 1965 to publicly criticize Chinese human rights abuses in Tibet. This report also drew the attention of the UN Commissioner for Human Rights (UNCHR), the most important UN human rights agency. In 1992, for the first time ever, the UNCHR began to regularly review human rights issues in Tibet.

Another UN organization, the United Nations High Commission for Refugees, has provided support for Tibetan refugees for many years. In addition, the United Nations Development Program recently provided funding to support ecotourism projects inside Tibet that will provide economic relief to one of Tibet's most impoverished regions. The project, undertaken in conjunction with the Chinese government, is designed to generate income for people living in a nature preserve on Mount Everest. The funding will also help protect the ecology and biodiversity of this picturesque mountain region and the culture and traditions of its Tibetan inhabitants.

forced to flee from Chinese border guards, but in the process, he nearly drowned crossing a turbulent river. Maykut asked the students if she could take the paintings and their stories back to the United States with her so that she could tell others about the plight of Tibetan refugees. The result was an exhibit of the paintings that appeared at the University of Minnesota's Bell Museum, at a Minneapolis YWCA, and at Marcy Open School in Minneapolis in late 1998.

OUTLOOK FOR THE FUTURE

Through the efforts of the Dalai Lama, other Tibetan officials, and grassroots awareness campaigns, more people than ever before know about the conflict in Tibet. Yet these efforts have focused more on human rights and less on the views that divide Tibet and China—namely, who governs Tibet and what are its borders. As a result, the increased public awareness has not translated into a peaceful settlement. Nor has it improved human rights conditions for the Tibetan people.

As China and Tibet continue to drift apart, a solution to the conflict is nowhere in sight. Although the Dalai Lama and other Tibetan leaders hope to reach a peaceful compromise, so far China has not been willing—nor has it deemed it necessary—to negotiate. Some day the Chinese and Tibetan leaders may resolve their differences. Until then, conflict will continue on the "Roof of the World." ⊕

Despite increased awareness and the sometimes violent controversy over Tibet's independence, Tibetan peasants (right) continue to farm and raise animals as their ancestors did.

© Dennis Cox/ChinaStock

EPILOGUE*

As 1999 came to a close, the Dalai Lama and Jiang Zemin had made no plans to negotiate an end to the conflict. The Dalai Lama's decision to meet with British Prime Minister Tony Blair in May 1999, soon after NATO bombed the Chinese Embassy in Belgrade during the campaign against Yugoslavia, drove the two sides even farther apart.

In June 1999 Gyaltsen Norbu, the Panchen Lama according to the Chinese government, returned to Lhasa and asked Tibetan Buddhists to obey Jiang Zemin and to honor the Chinese motherland. Observers believe that in moving the Panchen Lama back to Tibet, the PRC hoped to strengthen his position. One of the Panchen Lama's most important responsibilities is to choose the next Dalai Lama. Since the majority of Tibetan Buddhists refuse to accept the Panchen Lama put forth by Beijing, it is difficult to predict the outcome in the event of the Dalai Lama's death. In October 1999, Gedhun Choekhi Nyima, the Dalai Lama's choice for Panchen Lama, remained in a Chinese prison. The PRC still refused to disclose the boy's whereabouts and gave no indication that he would be released anytime soon.

Meanwhile, human rights organizations continued to cite the PRC for human rights abuses. In September 1999, the Tibetan Centre for Human Rights and Democracy, a group based in India, reported that a Tibetan monk named Ngawang Jinpa died at home from injuries inflicted upon him while in a Lhasa jail. He had been serving a 12-year sentence on charges that he had participated in counter-revolutionary activities.

*Please note: The information presented in *Tibet: Disputed Land* was current at the time of the book's publication. For late-breaking news on the conflict, look for articles in the international section of U.S. daily newspapers. *The Economist*, a weekly magazine, is another good source for up-to-date information. You may also wish to access the following Internet sites: <http://headlines.yahoo.com/full-coverage/world/Tibet> and <http//www.tibet.org/tibet100/DigJan97.html>.

CHRONOLOGY

600s Songtsen Gampo, ruler of the Tibetan kingdom, marries Princess Wengcheng of China.

630–800 Buddhism spreads throughout Tibet and comes to play a central role in Tibetan society.

763 The new Chinese emperor fails to pay the silk tribute. Tibet retaliates, capturing an important Chinese region and replacing the emperor with a puppet ruler favored by the Tibetan king.

800s–900s Tibet and China come to regard one another as equals.

821 Tibet and China sign the Treaty of Uncle and Nephew.

1042 Tibet experiences a period of renewal prompted by the arrival of Pandit Atisha, a Buddhist teacher from India.

1200s Mongol warlord Ghengis Khan threatens Tibetan stability but dies without invading Tibet.

1240 Godan Khan, grandson of Ghengis, invades Tibet and appoints Sakya Pandita, Tibet's most eminent lama, as vice regent of Tibet.

1279 Mongols subdue the Chinese, who despise their conquerors.

1368 The Chinese overthrow the Mongols and establish the Ming dynasty.

1642 Tibetans invite Gusri Khan, a Mongol prince, to visit Tibet.

1645 The Ming dynasty is unseated by the Qing dynasty.

1700s Sangye Gyatso forges a military alliance with Galdan Khan.

1706 Mongol troops kill Sangye Gyatso and arrest the Sixth Dalai Lama in Lhasa.

1723 China's emperor stations a civilian adviser in Tibet to replace Tibet's military governor and pulls Chinese troops out of Tibet.

1750 Representatives of China's emperor reorganize the Tibetan government. The Tibetan kingship is abolished and power is placed in the hands of the Dalai Lama.

1793 China again reorganizes Tibet's government and takes control over Tibet's communication with the outside world.

1796–1804 Political corruption spurs a series of anti-imperial rebellions.

1839–1842 China is at war with Britain. Britain eventually defeats China.

1851–1864 Chinese villagers wage the Taiping Rebellion against the government.

1894 Chinese-Japanese War.

1904 Sir Francis Younghusband invaded Tibet to defend British political and economic interests. The Anglo-Tibetan Convention is ratified at Simla, India, by Tibet and Britain but not by China.

1906 China and Britain sign the Anglo-Chinese Convention, effectively reversing the most important elements of the 1904 Convention.

1910 China's emperor marches on Tibet with 2,000 troops to take over the region for good.

1911 Revolution begins in China.

1912 Tibetan opposition groups expel Chinese troops from Tibet.

1913 The Thirteenth Dalai Lama formally declares Tibet's independence and breaks all ties with China. Britain supports Tibetan independence by organizing the Simla Conference.

1922 Refusing to pay taxes to support Tibet's military, the Panchen Lama has a falling out with the Dalai Lama and flees to China.

1933 The Thirteenth Dalai Lama dies.

1936 Japanese troops invade China.

1937 The Panchen Lama dies in China after the Chinese made numerous attempts to return him to Tibet.

1939 Tibetan monks choose a new Dalai Lama.

1947 Britain grants independence to India and bows out of Asian affairs.

1949 The Chinese Communist Party (CCP) topples the Nationalist government and gains control of China, creating the People's Republic of China (PRC).

1950 China launches a full-scale military assault on Tibet.

1951 The People's Liberation Army (PLA) quells the Tibetan military resistance. Under threat of further attacks, Tibetan negotiators sign the 17 Point Agreement, granting Chinese control over Tibet with the understanding that Tibet's political system would remain intact along with the Dalai Lama's authority.

1954 The Chinese change their policy with Tibet by allowing the Tibetan government to exist only as a puppet for Chinese authority. India signs the Sino-Indian Agreement, giving their military outposts, telegraph facilities, and rest houses in Tibet to the PRC. China invites the Dalai Lama and Panchen Lama to visit Beijing and tour other regions of China.

1957 Tibetan leaders from Amdo and Kham form the resistance group Chushi Gangdruk and raid Chinese military convoys. Chushi Gangdruk gains control of the area south of Lhasa.

1958 Tibet stages a massive rebellion against Chinese occupation.

1959 Chinese artillery shells land near the summer home of the Dalai Lama. About 17,000 Tibetan refugees, including the Dalai Lama, settle in India.

1963 The PRC establishes the Tibet Autonomous Region (TAR) and further alters Tibet's traditional economy. The Chinese close Tibet to foreign visitors.

1966 The Cultural Revolution begins in China.

1971 In an effort to stop rebellion, China allows Tibetans to wear traditional clothing and relaxes restrictions on travel and religious practices. Secret talks with the Dalai Lama begin.

1981 Chinese reopen 45 Tibetan monasteries and allow families to return to subsistence farming. The Law on Regional Autonomy for Minority Nationalities is passed.

1985 China appoints Wu Jinghua as head of the Tibetan Communist Party.

1988 The Dalai Lama speaks to the European Parliament announcing that he will accept less than full independence for Tibet. Violence erupts when 30 Tibetans march into the center of Lhasa to protest the Chinese cancellation of a visit by the Dalai Lama.

1990 The Chinese replace Wu Jinghua with reformer Hu Jintao. Hu becomes part of the CCP.

1992–1993 The Chinese open Tibet to outside investment.

1995 The Dalai Lama declares the discovery of the new Panchen Lama, Gedhun Choekyi Nyima. The Chinese government selects a different Panchen Lama, Gyaltsen Norbu, and takes Gedhun Choekyi Nyima into custody. Negotiations take a giant step backward.

1996 A popular Lhasa shopping district is bombed. Bombs damage the house of a lama reported to be a Chinese sympathizer and the main gate of the Communist Party headquarters.

1997 Chinese president Jiang Zemin repeats his conditions for engaging Tibet in negotiations.

1999 The Tibet Youth Congress stages a hunger strike at the UN building in Geneva, Switzerland.

SELECTED BIBLIOGRAPHY

Barber, Noel. *From the Land of Lost Content: The Dalai Lama's Fight for Tibet.* Boston: Houghton Mifflin, 1970.

Goldstein, Melvyn C. *The Snow Lion and the Dragon: China, Tibet, and the Dalai Lama.* Berkeley and Los Angeles, CA: University of California Press, 1997.

Grunfeld, Tom A. *The Making of Modern Tibet.* Armonk, NY: M.E. Sharpe, 1987.

Lopez, Donald S. Jr. *Prisoners of Shangri-La: Tibetan Buddhism and the West.* Chicago: The University of Chicago Press, 1998.

Peissel, Michel. *The Secret War in Tibet.* Boston: Little, Brown and Company, 1972.

Richardson, Hugh E. *Tibet and Its History.* Second Edition, Revised and Updated. Boulder, CO: Shambhala Publications, 1984.

INDEX

ABOUT THE AUTHOR

Peter Kizilos is an award-winning author and communications consultant who lives in Minneapolis, Minnesota. He has written articles for major state and national publications and several books, including *South Africa: Nation in Transition, Quebec: Province Divided* and, with Jackie Nink Pflug, *Miles to Go Before I Sleep: My Grateful Journey Back from the Hijacking of Egyptair Flight 648.* For his commitment to leadership in public affairs, Peter was named a Mondale Fellow by the University of Minnesota's Hubert H. Humphrey Institute of Public Affairs. Peter received his B.A., cum laude, from Yale University and an M.A. in area studies from the University of Michigan at Ann Arbor.

ABOUT THE CONSULTANT

Andrew Bell-Fialkoff, *World in Conflict* series consultant, is a specialist on nationalism, ethnicity, and ethnic conflict. He is the author of *Ethnic Cleansing,* published by St. Martin's Press in 1996, and has written numerous articles for *Foreign Affairs* and other journals. He is writing a book on the role of migration in the history of the Eurasian Steppe. Bell-Fialkoff lives in Bradford, Massachusetts.

SOURCES OF QUOTED MATERIAL

p. 17 Gyaltsen Norbu, Chairman of the Tibet Autonomous Region, Xinhua News Agency interview, August 6, 1997; p. 31 Hugh E. Richardson, *Tibet and Its History,* Boston: Shambhala, 1984; p. 41 Lee Feignon, *Demystifying Tibet: Unlocking the Secrets of the Land of the Snows,* Chicago: Ivan R. Dee, Inc.,1996, 112; p. 49 Loretta Tofani, "Inside Tibet: A Country Tortured: Reeducation Digs at Roots of a People's Heritage," *Philadelphia Inquirer,* 9 December 1966; p. 60 Associated Press, "Bomb at Government Offices Wounds 5 in Tibetan Capital," The *New York Times,* 30 December 1996, A2.